I0814585

PRAISE FOR THE GUIDES FOR THE PRAIRIE GARDENER SERIES

"The Prairie Gardener's series offers knowledgeable yet accessible answers to questions covering a broad range of topics to help you cultivate garden success. Get growing!" —Lorene Edwards Forkner, gardener and author of *Color In and Out of the Garden*

"This is a beautiful and incredibly well-written series of books on earth-friendly gardening. Lavishly illustrated, with photos in every segment, the books are a pleasure just to leaf through, but the accessible writing and level of expertise makes them essential to any gardener's library. Although they're geared to prairie gardeners, I found great information that transfers anywhere, including where I live, in the Sierra Foothills, and will enjoy them for years to come. Well-indexed, to help you find solutions to elusive problems. Highly recommended!" —Diane Miessler, certified permaculture designer and author of *Grow Your Soil!*

"All your gardening questions answered! Reading the Prairie Gardener's series is like sitting down with your friendly local master gardener. Delivers practical guidance that will leave you feeling confident and inspired." —Andrea Bellamy, author of *Small-Space Vegetable Gardens*

"[This] series comes in mighty yet digestible volumes covering popular topics like seeds, vegetables, and soil. These question-and-answer-styled books get to the root of the matter with Janet and Sheryl's unique wit and humour. Although each guide touches on regionally specific information, the wisdom of these seasoned gardeners applies to any garden, wherever it may be." —Acadia Tucker, author of *Growing Perennial Foods*

Also by Janet Melrose and Sheryl Normandeau

Guided Journal

The Houseplanter: Your Go-To Growing Journal

Guides for the Prairie Gardener

The Prairie Gardener's Go-To for Vegetables

The Prairie Gardener's Go-To for Pests & Diseases

The Prairie Gardener's Go-To for Seeds

The Prairie Gardener's Go-To for Small Spaces

The Prairie Gardener's Go-To for Soil

The Prairie Gardener's Go-To for Trees & Shrubs

The Prairie Gardener's Go-To for Fruit

The Prairie Gardener's Go-To for Perennials

The Prairie Gardener's Go-To for Herbs

The Prairie Gardener's Go-To for Grasses

JANET MELROSE &
SHERYL NORMANDEAU

Staying Alive

The Go-To Guide for Houseplants

TOUCHWOOD

TouchWood Editions
touchwoodeditions.com

Copy edited by Paula Marchese

Proofread by Meg Yamamoto

Designed by Tree Abraham

Typeset by Sara Loos

Photos by Janet Melrose and Sheryl Normandeau

CATALOGUING DATA AVAILABLE FROM LIBRARY AND ARCHIVES CANADA

ISBN 9781771514576 (print)

ISBN 9781771514583 (electronic)

TouchWood Editions acknowledges that the land on which we live and work is within the traditional territories of the Lkwungen (Esquimalt and Songhees), Malahat, Pacheedaht, Scia'new, T'sou-ke, and W̱SÁNEĆ (Pauquachin, Tsartlip, Tsawout, and Tseycum) peoples.

We acknowledge the financial support of the Government of Canada through the Canada Book Fund, and the province of British Columbia through the Book Publishing Tax Credit.

This book was produced using FSC®-certified, acid-free papers, processed chlorine free, and printed with soya-based inks.

Printed in China

29 28 27 26 25 1 2 3 4 5

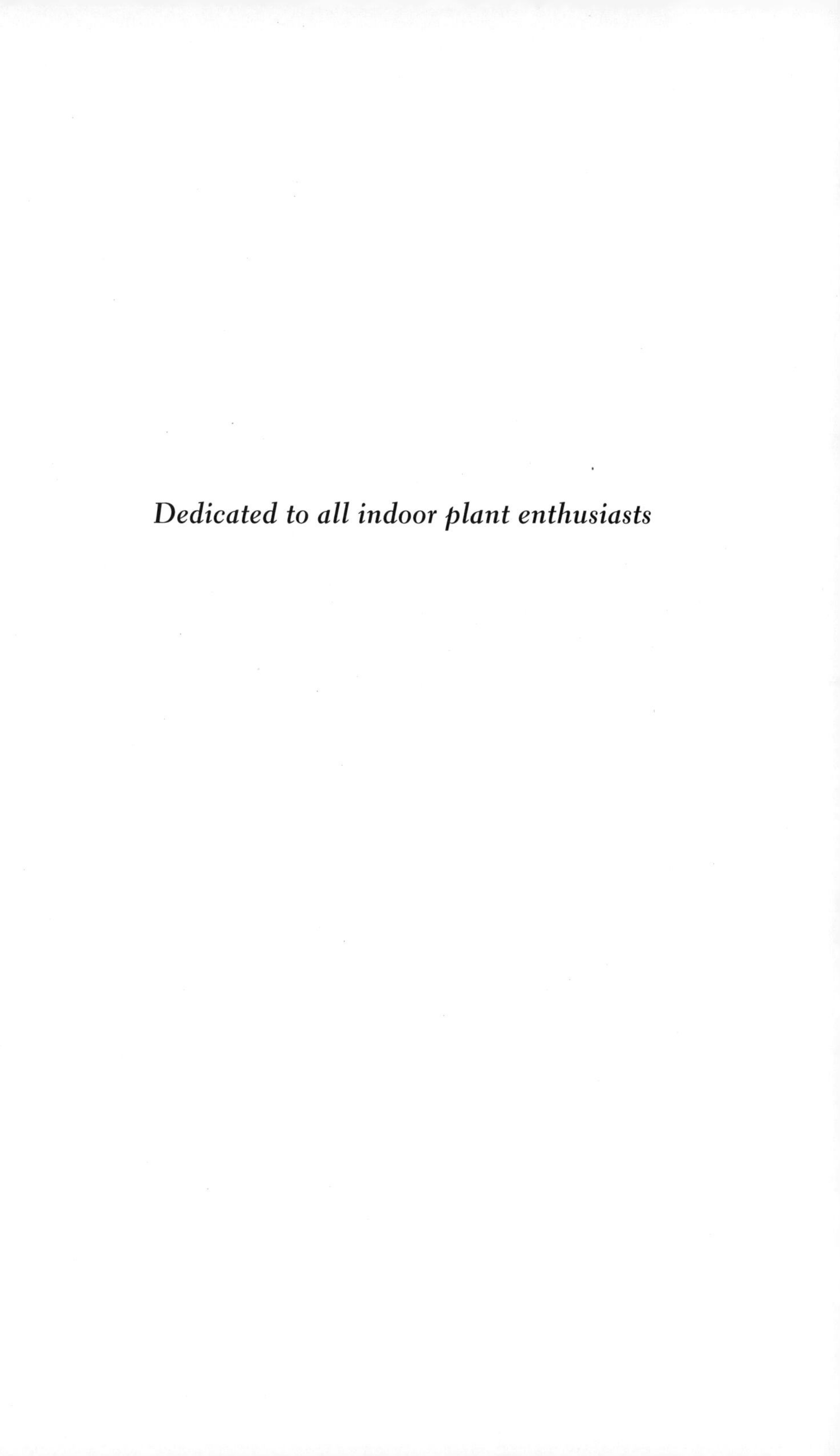

Dedicated to all indoor plant enthusiasts

Introduction

Whether you have one tiny succulent on your desk at work or a massive collection of tropical plants in your home, it's impossible to ignore the impact that caring for houseplants brings to our lives. We admire them for their beauty and uniqueness and the ways they decorate and define our living and working spaces.

The psychological benefits of houseplants cannot be understated either. As gardeners, we all know that warm, fuzzy feeling we get from nurturing plants. The act of caring for them—from watering to repotting—is deeply satisfying and can even reduce our stress levels. And horticultural therapists will tell you about the ways that having plants in a room will help with healing.

It's even more than that! Making more plants through propagation is extremely rewarding—especially when we can share the new plants with others. And if you're a dedicated houseplant collector, the thrill of finding a new cultivar you don't yet have can't be measured.

Should you get seriously bitten by the houseplant bug, like we are, then you have a lot of plants all happily competing for space in your place! Looking after them takes a bunch of know-how, the right equipment, and your enthusiasm. We are here to supply the know-how. You supply the rest! —SHERYL NORMANDEAU & JANET MELROSE

Need spice in your space? Liven up your decor with houseplants such as this vibrantly coloured croton.

Do plants clean the air indoors?

Back in 1989, NASA released a report of a study conducted under controlled conditions that stated that certain plants improve the air we breathe. Since then, it has been a commonly held belief that our indoor plants help improve the air quality in our homes.

The study did prove that plants can reduce certain pollutants in an enclosed space (for instance, space stations). Plants absorb carbon dioxide and release oxygen as part of the process of photosynthesis. They can also absorb some common volatile organic compounds (VOCs) such as formaldehyde, ozone, nitrous oxide, and carbon monoxide. But the problem is that they do so slowly. What they don't do is remove other common air quality problems such as mites, dust, allergens, and so on. Additionally, studies have found that you would need an awful lot of plants to make a difference to your air quality. Now, I have some one hundred plants in my small home, so perhaps they do make a difference. But in large homes, offices, and other indoor spaces, you probably would need a small forest to make a significant difference.

The reality is that if you open your windows for an hour on a nice day, that will be enough to refresh the air in your entire home. Which I do—even in the winter!

So, do we ditch houseplants as a bad idea? Not at all, as numerous studies—not to mention the experiences of ordinary people—testify to the positive benefits on our mental and physical health and well-being of having plants indoors.

So, we say, bring on the indoor plants and gardening. While they may not do a whole lot for our air quality, they positively help keep us sane in an increasingly fraught world. And there really isn't anything wrong with talking to them too![1] **—JM**

A living wall of any size can be a huge complement to a space, and it will boost your mental health, too!

Rooms to Grow: Designing with Houseplants

1

How do I know which types of indoor plants are suitable for my home?

It is oh so tempting to choose indoor plants based on what appeals to you at the store. But then you must figure out where to put them once they are home. It is a trap that I have fallen into many a time. They all look so great!

Much wiser is to learn the growing conditions in your home and choose plants that suit those conditions. Most homes will have many different environments, from dimmest corners to brightest windows. Humidity varies from room to room, with the kitchen and bathroom often the most humid. Temperatures can vary too, from cold windowsills to warm, steamy kitchens. What you choose might even come down to how warm or cool you like your home to be, as controlled by that battleground—the thermostat. Air conditioning or lack of it will affect your home's temperature too, especially during the hot months.

Plants placed in the wrong conditions are likely to struggle, yearning for that bright light or shivering in the cold. Stressed plants will stop growing or grow too fast. They will attract more pests, both insects and pathogens. They might even just call it a day and go to plant heaven.

It can be expensive to create the proper conditions for that *Plantum whydidibuyum* that looked so appealing in the store. It can also be expensive when they curl up their leaves and croak.

In our book *The Houseplanter: Your Go-To Growing Journal*, we describe many of our favourite plants and what conditions they really want to grow in. From ferns to cacti, monster tropical species to diminutive African violets, flowering plants to foliage ones, there are a multitude of choices for every corner.[1] A little research goes a long way toward avoiding mistakes and even steeling your mind to that plant that is trying to steal your heart.—JM

Tradescantia *(inch plants) are typically grown for their gorgeous foliage, but they will bloom when they are really,* REALLY *happy with their living arrangements.*

Is it better to buy an expensive large plant or a cheaper one in a smaller pot?

Going with the younger, smaller plant is usually the best option, actually. "More expensive" doesn't necessarily mean better; in fact, a smaller plant is easier to transport and will adapt more quickly to its new surroundings than a large one. And, if you're like me, you'll probably buy two plants to celebrate the cost savings. Am I right?[2] —**SN**

This diminutive panda plant (Kalanchoe tomentosa) *will eventually grow up to three feet (ninety centimetres) tall, but it's cuteness level at this stage is irresistible.*

Can I mix different houseplants together in a container?

For sure! To ensure success, there are some considerations with respect to requirements such as light, nutrients, and water. Your plant selections must be compatible; that is, you shouldn't pot up a drought-tolerant desert dweller with a dewy tropical. You'll never be able to adequately fulfill both of their needs for water and humidity. Likewise, a heavy feeder such as *Alocasia* won't be a suitable roommate for bird's nest fern (*Asplenium nidus*) or other plants that prefer lean soil.

Aesthetics matter, too! You'll want to showcase a collection of plants that look striking together, with different heights, leaf shapes, textures, and colours. The way you plant them will be a lot like arranging cut flowers, except you have to make allowances so that each plant receives the amount of light that it needs.

You may need to do a little research before you source the plants for your container, but once you find the right buddies, you'll be set! —SN

The varied textures in this container are bold and eye-catching! You'll notice the formula of "thriller, filler, and spiller" was used in the design.

Can we take our houseplants outside for the summer?

Absolutely! With certain conditions.

Every summer, usually around early June when the temperatures overall are around 60 to 65°F (15 to 18°C) and overnight temperatures are above 40 to 50°F (5 to 10°C), a lot of my houseplants go outside for their summer vacation. After a winter in lower light levels, plus dry and overly warm air, they positively flourish being outside until the coolness of September signals their return indoors. Not only do they receive extra energy from being outside, but the relatively higher humidity also improves their health, and the rain washes off dust and other pollutants from their leaves. They respond with a flourish of new growth as they grace my front porch and provide a great display under the shade of my huge spruce tree. I also use them in my outdoor containers, where they add a lot of panache.

Not all my indoor plants go outside. Those that are massive stay inside as they would likely get beaten up in windstorms and hail. Those that are fragile stay behind, as do those that don't appreciate the variability of our prairie summers. So, the monstera or Swiss cheese plant *(Monstera deliciosa)* stays safe inside where the hail won't add to its holes. Likewise, certain succulents like jade plant (*Crassula ovata)* or my various Christmas cacti (*Schlumbergera* spp.), who readily experience sunscald, stay behind. But pretty much everyone else goes out there.

Most of our houseplants won't appreciate direct sun, as they don't receive it in their native habitat nor are they exposed to it inside. Placing houseplants under a leafed-out deciduous tree or my spruce is ideal. Or in the shade of a building. They also won't like being where there are great winds to shred leaves or where they will experience some chilling damage. Do ensure that whichever containers they are in have lots of drainage holes as there is a good chance that at some point, they will get a monsoon or even a decent rain that would saturate the container if not for that drainage. You will also need to monitor the soil a fair amount and be prepared to water often on those hot, hot days. Make sure that you follow a good routine for fertilizing them over the summer with a full-strength liquid fertilizer or a slow-release granular fertilizer. Do also check for pests finding them, and be prepared to take any action required.

When it is time to go back inside, once temperatures are dipping overnight to less than 40°F (5°C), I always repot them with fresh potting soil. This gives them a nice boost for the return indoors, plus it reduces potential for insect eggs hatching later. Not a nice experience as I have variously found over the years if I take my chances and skip this step. It is a good idea to thoroughly wash the leaves, right into the nooks and crannies, and remove debris. Quarantine them for up to a month, if you can, so that you can monitor for any lingering pests.

Do be prepared for some sulking. No one is happy when the holidays are over, and you will likely see some plants experience leaf drop with the lower light levels. Resist pruning at this stage as the plants do not need any added stress at this point. Reduce the amount of water and strength of fertilizer accordingly, and allow them to settle back in to their old quarters. They will be happier now over the next few months as a result of their sojourn outside, and you get to welcome back in old friends.[3] —JM

If you want a tropical paradise on your deck or balcony, this is the way to accomplish it. Bring out the little umbrella drinks!

What is a moss pole? How would I use one?

Many of our houseplants such as monstera, philodendron, and pothos are epiphytes that grow on trees and shrubs in their natural habitat. Such plants provide the support and, in some instances, the means for the epiphytes' aerial roots to firmly attach, allowing them to climb upwards. As a rule, epiphytes sprawl if we don't give them a means of support.

Enter the moss pole. It is literally a stake, made of bamboo, a wooden dowelling, PVC piping, or anything handy at a length that will be appropriate for the plant. The stake is covered with moistened sphagnum moss, sheet moss, or even coir fibre. It is secured to the stake with string, jute, or fishing wire. A section of the pole at the bottom is bare of moss as it will be inserted into the depth of the plant pot. Making one can be messy but relatively simple. Use a tarp to catch the bits of moss or coir and wear gloves to protect your hands. You can also buy them premade.

Insert the stake next to the central stem of the plant, and gently train the plant to clamber up the pole. At first, you might need to use plant tape to secure the vines to the pole, but once they are firmly attached, the tape can be dispensed with. A moss pole is a great way to reduce the space a plant can take up and provides a more natural appearance for displaying your plant in your home.—**JM**

I want to train my trailing and vining plants along a wall. What can I use to mount them?

One of the most exciting parts about owning houseplants is showcasing them so that they look their best—after all, part of the reason why you have plants in the first place is to display how beautiful or unique they are! If you have some vining or climbing plants and you want to train them to climb up an interior wall, you have several options for mounting them so that they stay in place.

There are several types of hooks that will do the trick nicely. You can purchase clear plastic hooks that have adhesive strips strong enough to hold plant stems in place but can be removed at a later date without damaging the surface of the wall. Some people prefer to use decorative metal hooks and hang plant stems on them, using soft ties, covered wires, or even pipe cleaners. The key is not to use products that may pierce or bruise plant stems.

When you affix your plants to the wall, be careful not to force the stems into position. Plants such as philodendrons and pothos don't have stems that bend easily, so accommodate them by moving hooks (if you are using them) closer together.

Also, bear in mind that some plants will mark up the paint on your walls as they grow against them and deposit traces of tissue and sap. If a plant lives a long time, you may not be too upset about this, but if you have to move the plant or change decor for some reason, that wall may need some new paint. If you don't want this to happen, there are some beautiful wall-mounted trellises that you can put up. A plant can be trained to grow up the trellis using specialty trellis clips. The trellis provides a barrier between the wall and the plant.—SN

Golden pothos (Epipremnum aureum) *is an ideal candidate for mounting on a wall or indoor trellis.*

Home, Sweet Home: Choosing the Right Containers

2

How do I select containers for my houseplants?

One of the most important things you need to consider is drainage. Most houseplants do not tolerate sitting in pools of water and soggy soil. If you've found a gorgeous ceramic pot that you simply must have and it doesn't possess drainage holes, use a cache pot as a liner. The cache pot can be a plastic grower's pot, which has large holes in the base. Even if you use a cache pot, ensure that you don't allow the plant to sit in a puddle for too long. Lift the cache pot and drain the decorative pot after watering.

The size of the containers you choose for your plants is important, too. You're looking for the most comfortable size. If you're transplanting, don't get a giant container right off the bat. Your plant will not be happy, even if it will eventually grow to the size that large pot will hold. Transplant by increments. Yes, that means that you will have to purchase multiple containers, but hopefully you can repurpose them for other plants.

Your decor and personal style will also dictate the type of plant pots that you use. Your colour choices as well as the shapes of the pots reflect your tastes. Houseplant containers are made of a variety of materials, including clay, plastic, fibreglass, metal, wicker, ceramics, glass, wood, and more. The materials you choose will also complement your home's interior design.

Depending on the types of containers you purchase, it may be necessary to also buy saucers for them. The saucers can help with drainage as well as bottom watering. If you struggle with consistent watering, you can try a self-watering planter, which has a reservoir from which the water wicks up into the soil.

There are some specialty pots on the market, designed for specific types of plants. African violet pots are usually a self-watering style, with a fluted bowl shape that suits the plant's form. (Sometimes African violet pots rest on tiny decorative feet!) Orchid pots usually come with clear plastic liners, so that you can easily pull them out and inspect your plants' roots. (You can buy the liners separately and put them into your favourite pots.)

Plants that trail are well suited to hanging, and you have numerous choices when it comes to selecting containers. You can try a ceramic or plastic pot suspended with a macramé hanger (they're back in style and more beautiful than ever!) or a basket style like you would use outdoors.

Wall-mounted pots are great for small spaces. Decorative sconce styles or even window-box types can be attached to walls and offer a place for trailing or small plants. —**SN**

Let that hoya hang! This beauty can make a huge statement in a room if given the right container and conditions.

What is a Wardian case and how does it apply to houseplants?

The Wardian case is a piece of botanical history with practical applications for today's indoor gardeners.

Back in the 1800s, plant explorers went all over the world collecting plant species that were new to Europe, but they lacked a method to get the new specimens home alive. Only 1 out of 1,000 plants might make it home in any shape to be studied, never mind being propagated, considering the long overseas travel time with lack of fresh water or optimal light.

Botanists had been trying to find ways to get their plants home, but it was by accident that in 1829, amateur naturalist Dr. Nathaniel Bagshaw Ward placed a moth chrysalis on a bed of moss in a glass jar and screwed on the lid. Well, the moth didn't emerge, but the moisture in the moss was contained in the jar, and spores of the moss and seeds of grass germinated and grew. Ward exposed the jar to light, and for three years the plants grew happily without receiving extra water.

It was an invention that changed the study of botany and fuelled the Golden Age of Horticulture in Europe. Wardian cases, big and small, were created to easily transport plants around the world, changing plant exploration and world trade as well.

Well, that is nice, you say, but how does that apply to me, a modern-day indoor gardener?

Given that our houses generally have low humidity, keeping those plants that enjoy high humidity alive can be almost impossible. For instance, I love maiden-hair ferns (*Adiantum* spp.) but could never keep them alive for long before I got a Wardian case for them to live in. Now they flourish indoors as do other high-humidity plants.

A Wardian case is a simple construction, though very fanciful. Ornate cases were initially created and are still available. Think of a small greenhouse, with the frame made of either wood or other materials such as lead, and glass panels installed and sealed in the frame. Usually, access to the case is via a lid rather than doors, and the idea is that you seldom need to open the lid once your plants are inside. You can buy one already made or make one from an old fish tank or open-top terrarium. Even a rose bowl works. Just make sure that you have a pane of glass on top (or glass plate in the case of a rose bowl), to make sure that moisture doesn't escape.

To create your Wardian case planter, line the bottom with 1 inch (2.5 centimetres) of gravel. Top it with a layer of sphagnum moss and then ¼ inch (6 millimetres) of charcoal. Top with 2 inches (5 centimetres) of potting mix and water to moisten. About two-thirds of the case should be open air. Then transplant your plants into the soil layer, using a tablespoon (15 millilitres) of water around each one. Close the case, and monitor to see if a little bit of condensation forms on the inside of the glass, and if the plants are looking happy. If there is no condensation and the plants are wilting or droopy, add a bit more water and keep monitoring. If there is a lot of condensation, then there is too much water in the system. Open the case and allow things to air out and dry out a bit, then resume monitoring. Once the system is running well, place the case in bright but indirect light. You do not want direct sun falling on the glass as it will crisp the plants inside. The case should not need to be opened except for tending the plants every so often, and be sure to do so quickly.

Then enjoy your Wardian case and your lovely ferns, mosses, and other plants inside.[1]—JM

What are terrariums?

The inventor of the Wardian case (see pages 26–27), Dr. Nathaniel Bagshaw Ward, published a book, *On the Growth of Plants in Closely Glazed Cases,* in 1842. In it, he espoused the benefits of using Wardian cases as well as early versions of terrariums, which could house moisture-loving plants. (A Scottish botanist named A.A. Maconochie had actually created the first terrarium in the 1830s, but since he didn't publish his findings, his work was never publicly acknowledged.)

Inspired by the success of the Wardian case, terrariums and vivariums (enclosed cases used for plants, reptiles, and amphibians) were popular in Victorian homes in the nineteenth century. Our modern aquariums, containing fish and sometimes live plants, were also created based on these designs.

Terrariums are glass containers—bottles, bowls, aquariums, and purpose-built terrarium cases, among other things—that contain soil and plants. Closed terrariums are sealed, although you can access the plants when needed through a hinged door. Open terrariums usually have one side that is not sealed.

Terrariums are largely self-sustaining, requiring only periodic watering. Within the confines of a glass case, water is constantly recycled: it is released as vapour, which condenses on the inside of the glass and provides moisture to plants. The environment within a terrarium is constantly damp, making it particularly hospitable for plants such as ferns and air plants.[2]—**SN**

How do you plant a terrarium?

The most difficult part of planting a terrarium is positioning plants within an enclosed space, especially if the terrarium is very small. You can purchase specialty tools such as forks and tweezers that are helpful when setting it up.

Your growing medium is the first thing that goes into a terrarium. Some growers like to place a layer of small gravel at the base of the container, but you don't have to. Next up: put down a layer of horticultural or terrarium charcoal. This layer helps with drainage and filtration. Add a layer of potting soil on top of the charcoal. How much soil you use depends on how large your terrarium is. Your plants will likely be small, without substantial root balls, but when you place your plants in the terrarium, the first layer of soil should cover at least half of the root balls.

Now for the fun part! Make sure you eye the scale of your terrarium, and add some decorative elements, such as large rocks or driftwood. The plants come next. Gently tease them into place, ensuring their root systems are fully in contact with the soil layer. Add more soil around each plant so that the root balls are covered. Finish up by misting the interior of your terrarium with distilled water in a spray bottle.

Your terrarium will need a source of light to keep your plants happy and healthy. Either natural sunlight or artificial light are suitable. Don't put the terrarium in direct, hot sunlight, or you will end up cooking your plants. Filtered light is always best. —**SN**

How do I care for a terrarium?

A terrarium is wonderfully low maintenance, but it still requires some inputs to ensure that the plants inside will thrive. Adhering to a regular watering schedule is essential, but not particularly onerous.

An open terrarium can be watered every three weeks. If you notice that plants are drying out too much, step up that timeline. A closed terrarium should be watered every four to six weeks. Once your terrarium is established, you'll be able to judge its watering requirements and can adjust, if needed.

You may not want to use a watering can to irrigate your terrarium plants, as one big accidental glug can wreak havoc with the ecosystem. Many terrarium owners choose to mist their plants using distilled water. (Why distilled water, you ask? It doesn't have any impurities that can upset the balance and aesthetics of your terrarium.)

Terrarium plants do not need much fertilizer to be happy. This is not a "go big or go home" scenario. If you apply too much fertilizer, it is nearly impossible to correct your mistake. Once a month, use a liquid fertilizer diluted to quarter strength. If you choose, you can use slow-release pellets instead.

Select slow-growing plants for your terrarium, so that they don't rapidly outgrow their habitat and, at the least, need trimming, or, at the worst, need rehoming. Trimming the plants in your terrarium will be a regular duty—you'll need to remove dead leaves or prune away dead stems to keep your plants looking their best. A pair of scissors is useful for this job.

Monitor your terrarium on a regular basis so that you can act should you notice detrimental insect activity or evidence that things just aren't humming along as they should.—**SN**

My terrarium plants are outgrowing their terrarium. How do I keep them small?

Plants grow when they are in a terrarium. It's a fact of life, and unless you chose dwarf ones or varieties that take a long time to outgrow their space, every so often you will need to do some pruning or transplanting.

Clues that you need to act include foliage touching the sides of the terrarium, plants growing over the top of the terrarium, or reaching the ceiling of a closed terrarium. Other hints are overcrowding in the terrarium, when you can't see the plants through the forest of foliage. Ailing plants are another sign to get moving, as their roots might have overtaken the growing medium supporting them, and there simply aren't enough nutrients or air in the system to keep them healthy.

The best time to address problems is at the beginning of the growing season. Do avoid pruning in the winter, if you can, as plants will take longer to recover if they are in dormancy.

Do an assessment to see whether a little judicious pruning back will rectify things. Or do whole plants need to be taken out? Or perhaps the whole terrarium needs a makeover?

If it is a matter of a plant or two getting a bit rambunctious, then snip stems down to a more compact shape. If it's a branching plant, make sure you trim as close to a leaf axil as possible. If your plant grows from a crown, then snip the overly long stems down to just above the crown. This technique also works if stems are losing some leaves and looking untidy. Using long-handled scissors such as aquatic scissors or aquatic tweezers will help you get to where you need to in the terrarium so that you can do precise cuts.

If plants are overcrowding the terrarium, assess to see if you have too many, and if removing one or two will solve the problem. Sometimes a plant might benefit from being divided, in which case you can lever it out of the terrarium, split it apart, and replant one of the divisions in the terrarium. Now, you have an extra plant to start another terrarium or give away.

Plants that are growing well but are really wanting to be too large for the environment they are in should be removed and repotted into a larger container. There is no point in repeatedly pruning them back into shape. They will weaken from too much pruning and eventually give up the ghost.

If you decide that the only solution is to rejuvenate the terrarium, then gently tease out the plants from the growing medium. Assess each one as to whether it belongs back inside. If so, then prune it into shape and return it to the terrarium. Should you decide that one or more need to grow outside the terrarium, now is the chance to select new plants that are dwarf varieties, slow growing, or naturally low growing.

Once your plants are back in tip-top shape, refrain from encouraging excessive growth by fertilizing very minimally and pruning judicially before growth gets out of hand.—**JM**

When should I repot my plants?

All houseplants benefit from annual repotting, be they big or small. Over the course of the year, houseplants will have extracted all of the nutrients out of their growing medium, whether or not you have been fertilizing regularly. The organic matter will have broken down and been consumed, with the potting soil becoming compacted. This is noticeable when you water and it runs out of your pots easily and isn't readily absorbed back into the medium. In all likelihood, plants will have grown somewhat—sometimes a lot—and are at risk of becoming root-bound. Plants may even sink into their pots as the organic matter disappears. It is a great time to do a bit of pruning and training of your plants too while you are at it!

The best time to repot those plants is in the early spring, just before they get ready for the burst of growth to come. Be prepared with new pots, if desired, plus growing medium enriched with a slow-release fertilizer. I like to add a bit of activated charcoal too, to promote aeration. A nice warm spring day is ideal when I can be outside and

*This Chinese evergreen (*Aglaonema *spp.) is currently looking full and healthy, but there's a lot of density going on in that pot. It may need a transplant soon.*

make a mess. I take each plant in turn, loosen it from its pot, shake off some of the growing medium, examine roots to ensure they are healthy, divide the plant if it is getting too big for its britches or do a bit of discreet pruning, and then replant it into that lovely, fresh growing medium. Once replanted, I set each pot into a sinkful of water to soak up the water into the soil and then replace it into its saucer.

You might think that plants would sulk a bit after all that handling, but they love it and will gladly put on that burst of growth as your reward.

If, with the press of life, you miss the annual repotting extravaganza, then watch for plants that have their roots growing out of the bottom, or heaving out, of their pots. Both are shout-out-loud notices that these plants should be repotted. Other calls to action are if plants are top-heavy and falling over, or if there is a buildup of salts on the surface of the growing medium or on the insides of pots, or if water is pooling on the surface of the growing medium or if it has pulled away from the sides of pots. Should plants be growing not at all or very slowly with weak stems and foliage, then that too is a good indicator that repotting will be welcomed.

I like to think of repotting as my plants' annual health check. We all love it![3]—JM

What is root pruning and when should I do it?

Root pruning sounds very scary, indeed. But it can be necessary if an indoor plant becomes root-bound, especially if girdling roots are strangling the plant. A root-bound plant has trouble with taking up nutrients and water, and you will see signs of stress with yellowing leaves and possibly the whole root ball being heaved out of the pot.

To start with, remove the plant from the pot onto a tarp. Then cut off the outer layer of soil and roots, especially those circling the pot. Next, loosen up the soil around the roots, and assess the situation. Once you know which roots can be readily removed, sever them cleanly with a sterilized blade. It is usually safe to remove up to one-third of the root ball for most plants.

Follow up by repotting the plant in the same (or a slightly larger) container, keeping the plant in the same position in the container. Add fresh, pre-moistened potting soil on the bottom of the pot and around the roots.

Water the plant, replace it in its location, and monitor it for signs of stress. Hold back the fertilizer for a couple of weeks while it is re-establishing itself.

You will find that the plant will look happier almost immediately.—JM

Light, Water, Action!

3

What are the light requirements for houseplants?

We tend to buy our indoor plants for their attractiveness, be it their foliage, flowers, size, or just that cuteness factor. We presume that our homes have the light needed for our plants to thrive, because they appear light enough to us. We know that our north-facing rooms are gloomier if the lights aren't on, and that the sun shining through those west-facing kitchen windows can be sunny, hot even.

The trick though is what kind of light and for how long does each of our plants prefer and, indeed, need for photosynthesis. A cactus from the desert is going to need different levels of sunlight than that tropical used to living in the canopy of a rainforest. If both are on the same shelf, chances are someone—maybe both plants—is not going to be happy. The result is often a slow decline in health and eventual death. The plants literally are starving (for light). People often say that they can't keep a plant alive in their homes. Chances are that this is largely due to the light they provide for their plants.

Understanding how light works as energy for photosynthesis is often explained through foot-candles, a measurement of the intensity of natural light. A foot-candle (FC) is the intensity of a candle 1 foot (30 centimetres) away from the plant. As a guide, outside in the direct sun, there are 10,000 foot-candles of light. Inside our homes, the deepest, darkest corner may have 50 foot-candles. Quite the difference!

Indoors, foot-candles range from that 50 FC to upwards of 8,000 FC. Those plants on a windowsill with full-on direct sunlight receive 8,000 FC, which is often described as bright, direct, high, or intense sunlight. The duration of time that they receive that amount of light also counts. If it's just for an hour, that cactus won't be happy, but the tropical one can survive and thrive when the light becomes more subdued and reduces towards 1,000 FC—bright, indirect light—as the sun moves away. Direct light can be filtered as well through curtains, blinds, or even the foliage of a tree outside.

Away from the window, the light intensity reduces dramatically toward the 200 FC range. Often described as indirect or medium light, many tropical plants can live happily with such light. Low light is light below 200 FC.

The light requirements found on many tags at the store are generally a decent guide to the type of light a plant prefers. If the plants do not receive that ideal amount of light, they may be healthy, but they are likely not growing by leaps and bounds. Sometimes that is okay as plants will be manageable with slower growth. If your plants are looking sickly, though, losing colour in their leaves, being prone to pests, and generally looking miserable, you can bet that the intensity of light or amount of it is not what it needs.

Using a light meter, which are readily available, can tell you exactly how many foot-candles of light there are in any spot in your home. They are a scientific way of gauging the light that a new plant needs so that it finds its proper home right from the get-go. Using a light meter is an eye-opener for most of us as we switch from our people view of light to that of how plants perceive light. After all, light is the stuff of life for them. Best that we be good plant parents and give them the right amount, for the right amount of time, plus time for rest at night.[1] —JM

Pothos are one of the most forgiving houseplants around when it comes to light: they truly don't need a lot of sunlight to be content. For many other houseplants, however, you'll need to very carefully consider where you are siting them and if they need supplemental light.

What types of grow lights are best for houseplants?

No matter the natural lighting in your home, there are likely some spots where you would like to have plants but the light is too low for what you want to be there.

Enter grow lights. These are full-spectrum lights that mimic natural sunlight, emitting blue and red light that is the best wavelength for photosynthesis. The light appears white to us but not to plants. The light being emitted isn't as strong as sunlight but is perfectly adequate for our indoor houseplants.

Depending on the type of grow lights you get, they will emit light in the 400 to 700 nanometre range, which is ideal for plant growth. Many are between 5,000 and 6,500 Kelvin and are most effective. Some lights are sold as T5 or T8, with T5 having the higher wattage for a greater intensity of light. (The "T" refers to the tubular shape of the bulb.) Look at the packaging for this information as it will tell you a lot about the particular light being sold.

There are four different types of grow lights: incandescent, fluorescent, light-emitting diode (LED), and high-intensity discharge (HID). These days, the most efficient lights, both for your electricity bill and for the light being shone on your plants, are LEDS or HIDS. These two types of lights can be placed close to your plants because they don't emit too much heat, which can scorch leaves.

HID lights are usually meant for commercial operations and have really high light intensity. Perhaps not what you need in your home. On the other hand, LED lights have become very affordable and come in a variety of styles that can be aesthetically pleasing as well as doing a beautiful job for your plants.

I use gooseneck LED lights. The lights come inserted in bendable "necks," so that I can position the lights at just the right angle. Mounted on long (or short for table-top) standards, they have become part of my decor. I also use traditional grow lights that hang from a crossbar. Not quite so decorative, but when I have lots of plants wintering indoors, it is a great way for them to get that light without fuss and bother.

The lights should be placed about a foot (thirty centimetres) away from the foliage so that the light can spread to cover the whole plant and ensure that the leaves do not burn. You can reduce the intensity of light by placing the lights farther away or higher overhead, as some tropical plants do not require that much light. You can also use grow lights together with natural light to great effect.

Plants entirely lit by grow lights will typically need between sixteen and eighteen hours of illumination. Those with access to some natural light do beautifully with twelve to sixteen hours of light. The timers that come with many lights make it a breeze to maintain light duration without trying to remember to turn them off and on. What plants don't need is light twenty-four hours a day. They need a rest period, just like we do![2]—JM

I use tap water to water my plants. Should I let it sit before using it? What about using filtered, distilled, hard, and soft water?

You would think that water (H_2O) would be a simple matter. But water is rarely just water. It naturally contains minerals in varying amounts as well as bacteria. It also has a pH factor that can affect the growth of plants, if it is too high or too low.

The closest that we can get to pure water is distilled water. Distilled water doesn't contain heavy metals, chemicals, impurities, or living organisms such as bacteria. To create it, water is boiled, then the vapour is distilled and bottled. Using distilled water exclusively on your houseplants means that you'll never have an issue with salt buildup from water (salts from fertilizer is another matter entirely), and you won't have to worry about water being a source of chemicals, such as chlorine and fluoride. Choosing to use distilled water may depend on your budget, however, as it is expensive. As well, you will need to compensate for the lack of minerals by keeping up with regular applications of fertilizer (which you're doing anyway, right?).

Tap water has been treated with chlorine, chloramines, and algicides to render it safe for us to drink. It still contains the normal amount of minerals and pH of untreated water. If water is used straight from the tap to water plants, the chlorine and other chemicals can cause stunted growth as well as yellowing leaves of sensitive plants.

As gardeners, we have been told that we should leave tap water out for twenty-four hours so that the chlorine will gas off. Unfortunately, very little chlorine in our water is in a free state, which encourages gassing off. The balance is tied up with other chemicals to form chloramines that will remain in the water no matter how long we wait to use it. To get rid of those molecules, we recommend using a dechlorinator, which can be purchased from fish stores.

Filtered water is usually run through an activated charcoal filter or a reverse osmosis filter, which removes chlorine as well as organic compounds such as pesticides, trichloroethylene (TCE), and heavy metals such as arsenic. Like distilled water, filtered water will have a lot of the natural minerals removed, so a regular fertilization schedule will be needed to offset the removal of those minerals.

Hard water contains a fair amount of calcium and other minerals such as magnesium. Most water softeners use resin beads with sodium carbonate that remove the calcium and magnesium, replacing them with sodium and potassium. Softened water causes a buildup of salts in the growing medium, which is harmful to plants.

Considering all the factors, we believe that filtered water is the best option for your plant's health outside of rainwater, but you need to factor in the additional costs of these products.

A final note: Fish water contains all those lovely nitrates and other nutrients. If you have an aquarium, please use that water for your plants.[3] —JM & SN

Alocasias, such as this 'Yellow Tail' cultivar, prefer evenly moist soil. They cannot tolerate boggy or bone-dry conditions. As the owner of this beauty, you'll need to strike a careful balance when you water to ensure your plant receives the best care.

I have heard that it is a good idea to water my plants with cold tea. Is that correct?

As someone who drinks scads of tea every week, I have grown up with this old wives' tale that we should water our plants with leftover tea. But I have never bothered.

Certainly, dried tea leaves (as well as coffee grounds and other greens we consume) contain amounts of nitrogen, phosphorus, and potassium as well as other chemicals, some of which are micronutrients for plants. Tea also contains fluorine, aluminum, manganese, and other minerals, some of which can retard plant growth. Black tea has a pH of about 5.5, which might be good to counteract the higher pH of regular tap water, if used consistently, but herb and green teas have a neutral pH.

Studies have found that the percentages of macronutrients in tea leaves, when diluted into tea, are about the same as those found in many fertilizers for indoor use, if diluted properly.

While it might be tempting to use leftover tea for your plants as a substitute fertilizer, given the presence of other chemicals, including pesticides, and the potential for growth retardation, it seems a dodgy idea. It's better to use a fertilizer that is purpose-made for plants.

Though if you happen to have a cup leftover in the pot, and you use it to occasionally water your plants, it won't hurt them, and it's better than dumping it. Be sure to compost those leaves, though![4]—**JM**

Can I use rainwater or melted snow to water my houseplants?

Yes, to both—as long as you find clean sources for them. When you harvest water from nature (whether it is in liquid form or more on the solid side), it will contain minerals that are beneficial to plants. Depending on the site of collection, however, the water may also have accumulated impurities or contaminants that could affect plant health. For example, you're not going to want to gather snow that was pushed off a sidewalk caked in ice-melt products and use it to water your plants.

It goes without saying, but if you choose to use snow for your houseplants, bring it into the house to warm and melt it first. You don't want to heap it onto your plants when it is in its icy form. Likewise, rainwater should be left to reach room temperature before using it on your plants.—SN

Twisted bird's nest fern (Asplenium antiquum) *can't handle waterlogged soils, but drought makes it pout.*

I have killed plants in the past with too much water. What is the best way to water houseplants?

I suspect that the greatest enemy our houseplants face isn't a mealybug army or a curious cat but rather the watering can (or, more accurately, the person wielding it). Many of us have a heavy hand when it comes to watering. I'm not sure if it has anything to do with the philosophy of "more is better," but chronic overwaterers need to take things back a few notches.

Most houseplants do not thrive in consistently damp growing mediums; they prefer to dry out between waterings. (Exceptions include moisture-loving ferns.) Test your growing medium to make sure you actually need to water. You can use a moisture meter, which you can purchase at most big-box stores or plant shops. Or you can simply plunge your finger down to the second knuckle into the soil. If the soil feels damp, you can wait a bit longer to water. As mentioned on pages 48–49, the length of time between waterings can vary, depending on the time of year and the type of containers your plants are living in.

Underwatering can also be a significant problem. You need to aim for "just right," which you can do by bottom watering (see page 48). —SN

Maidenhair ferns like consistently damp conditions, but you'll find that many of your houseplants are not in the same boat. The key to being a good houseplant guardian is to know and properly respond to the individual needs of your plants.

How do I water my bromeliads?

There are several types of bromeliads, with various types of growth habits, leaf shapes, and colours. Many varieties that we have access to as houseplant growers have large broad leaves arranged in a rosette, forming a cup-like structure at the base. In the same way you pour water into the reservoir of a coffee maker, bromeliads are irrigated by collecting water in that leaf cup. I'm not going to lie. The first time someone told me how to properly water these fascinating plants, I was taken aback: Surely that invites rot? Not for this plant! In their native habitat in the rainforests of Central and South America, these plants collect rainwater and take it up from their centre cups as needed. I am particularly enthralled with this set-up as it means I don't have to haul out the watering can as often.

One thing to bear in mind when watering bromeliads is that they're used to high-quality water (rainwater in a rainforest is pretty decent stuff), so avoid using hard water. Filtered water is best, if you have the means to process it (see page 42).—**SN**

Bottoms up for bromeliads!

I forget to water my houseplants! Is there a way to prevent this?

As houseplant growers, we sometimes struggle to maintain the balance between watering our green babies too much and watering them too little. Sometimes we fail to pay attention to their individual needs, assuming that all plants in our collection need the same amount of water on the same schedule. Sometimes we simply get busy, and next thing you know, three weeks have flown by, and some of our leafy dependants are no longer looking their finest. If forgetting to water is an issue for you, there are a few things you can do to compensate.

1. We are tooting our own horns here, but we have a lovely companion book (*The Houseplanter: Your Go-To Growing Journal*) that can help you keep track of your houseplant watering schedule.
2. Create a watering schedule on your favourite electronic device. There are a few apps you can peruse and try out on a trial basis, but you can also just set up notifications in a calendar. Remember to tailor the schedule to cover the needs of all the different types of houseplants you own.
3. When you water, take your time and ensure that every plant gets a good saturating drink. You don't want to make a mud puddle, but you want the soil to be thoroughly moist. Dribbling is nice in basketball, but your plants need more than that. The plant pots should feel heavy when you're done watering. If your containers have sufficient drainage and your growing medium is porous, filled with pockets of air, your plants' roots will be healthy. Happy roots = happy plants. If you water like this, your plants will not dry out quickly.
4. Water from the bottom. For this to be successful, your containers must have drainage holes so that the water can be taken up from the saucers that your plants are ideally residing in and can be wicked into the soil. When watering from the bottom, plants should not sit in a pool of water for too long, as root rot can be a result. If you water from the bottom, empty any leftover water in the saucers after an hour has passed.

Remember that if the temperature inside your home is high, your plants may need more frequent watering. If your plants are root-bound in their containers and are wilting or possibly yellowing, they are letting you know that you need to water them more often. The types of containers you are growing your houseplants in may also dictate your watering schedule: If unglazed terracotta is something you love to use as a plant habitat, extra watering sessions may be necessary as the clay dries out quickly. Plastic, ceramic, resin, or glazed clay containers are good alternatives and help hold the moisture in the soil better.

In the winter months, you won't need to water your houseplants as frequently as during the spring and summer, since there is less light coming into the house.[5] —SN

Shower with your plants!

Well . . . not quite. Take them into the shower, however, and very gently give them a rinse with tepid water. You can flush out some mineral salts this way as well as increase humidity for those that love that, and thoroughly water them, to boot.—SN

Rex begonias, such as this delightful cultivar 'Escargot', thrive in high humidity.

How do water globes work? Is the hype true—do they take the worry out of watering plants?

Those glass globes are very attractive, and so is the rationale that is made about them. The proposition is that when you use water globes, which is a form of water diffusion, you will have worry-free watering for your plants.

As always, there is no such thing as a free lunch, and water globes have their pros and cons. The main claim for water globes is that they supply water on a constant basis, and that all you need to do is fill them up every week to two weeks, and you are done. Nothing could be further from the truth!

A water globe is hollow, with a round bulb at the end and a long, skinny tube that is inserted into the soil mixture. Pre-moisten your soil and make a channel with a pencil for the tube to slide into. Fill the globe three-quarters full, tip the globe upside down, and quickly insert the tube deep into the soil in the pot. Once the globe is positioned in the pot, a bit of water will trickle out of the tube and air will go in to create a weak vacuum so that the water won't rush out all at once. As the soil in the container dries out, more air will flow into the globe and water will escape, and hopefully provide continually moist soil that isn't too wet for your plant.

You will need to monitor the globe and soil moisture to find out how long the water will last in the globe, and whether the amount provided is enough to keep the soil moist enough for the needs of your plant. More than one globe may be needed if you have a large container or a plant that needs lots of water. Once you have those variables figured out, then you can settle into a rhythm and be confident that your plant has what it needs water-wise.

Each time you fill the water globe, you will need to unclog the soil from the tube, using a pipe cleaner or other slender brush. If the globe is starting to look cloudy or you can see algae growing inside, rinse it out with a mixture of vinegar, lemon juice, baking soda, and a bit of dish soap. It is a good idea to do so at least every second time you refill the globe to prevent problems.

Given the work involved in monitoring, cleaning, and refilling the globes, the question becomes: Are they worth it?

The reality is that thcy arc not a time saver, nor the answer for those of us who forget to water our plants, or wait to do so until they droop. Though they are a good device to prevent overwatering and having water overflowing the catch tray and going all over the floor!

Whether to use water globes depends on the plants in question. For those plants that require their soil to almost totally dry out before being watered, water globes are the wrong thing to use. (Plants that prefer their soil to not be totally dry before being rehydrated can use water globes as supplemental moisture before regular waterings.) For plants that need consistently moist soil, water globes can be a plant saver, not just to keep them from dying, but for their overall health.

Water globes can also be a lifesaver for your plants if you go away for a few days and you don't trust someone with watering those loved plants.

The bottom line is that water globes are a tool to use in your plant-watering regime. They can't—and should not—replace all watering, but, if used effectively, they can assist with ensuring that you have healthy and happy plants.[6]—JM

What are moisture sensors? How are they used?

Moisture sensors measure humidity in soil. There are several types to choose from, and they work with varying degrees of accuracy. An analog moisture meter has a long metal probe that you plunge about three-quarters of the way into the growing medium. Don't push the probe against the base of the container or the reading will be inaccurate. A meter at the top of the probe measures the humidity of the soil on a scale of one to ten, with one being very dry and ten being very wet.

A battery-operated digital meter works in the same way, except that, in addition to soil moisture, it offers more measurements, such as soil pH and light levels. Some models also include a digital guide that offers information about common houseplants and their specific watering requirements.

Then there are the more rustic types of moisture sensors, made from terracotta and other types of clay. These often come in fun shapes, such as little earthworms. All you do is push the sensor into the growing medium and enjoy it as an ornament. When the soil is wet, the clay will be a dark colour; when the soil is dry, the clay will also dry out and be light in colour.

Do you need to have a moisture sensor for your houseplants? No, but if you worry about how often to water, these gadgets can be useful. Plus, some of us simply like playing with little gizmos like these, and they're not prohibitively expensive. You can always ask for one for a gift! —**SN**

Do orchids need to be watered with ice cubes?

For such a chilly subject, this is one question that has been hotly debated for years. The idea that owners of *Phalaenopsis* orchids should water their plants with three ice cubes once a week seems utterly ridiculous: Why the heck would we put ice near plant tissues? It seems like a deadly notion. Yet many *Phalaenopsis* growers swear by it, claiming that it solves the problem of underwatering their plants. *Phalaenopsis* are usually grown in a bark mix, which can easily dry out. These orchids cannot tolerate a lack of water (nor can they suffer overwatering), so a consistent, regular watering schedule is key. Someone realized that the equivalent of three ice cubes was the correct amount of water, and once a week was the proper time to deliver it, and the controversy has raged ever since.

But recent scientific research has given us an answer: in a study conducted by the Ohio State University and the University of Georgia, it was discovered that ice cubes don't damage orchid roots (when the plants are grown in bark and the ice cubes are placed on the bark surface), and most *Phalaenopsis* species actually receive the correct amount of water if they are given three ice cubes per week. You shouldn't hold an ice cube against an orchid's aerial roots for any length of time, but who would do that anyway? Ice cube waterers, you have my permission to proceed![7]—**SN**

It's vacation time, and I have no one to come and water my plants. Do you have any tips for me?

If this is a summer vacation, and your space is already hot, move your plants away from windows where they are exposed to direct sunlight. Add a 1-inch (2.5-centimetre) layer of pebbles (easily acquired at a pet store that sells fish supplies) to the saucers beneath your plant pots. This is one time you should not add water directly to the saucers; instead, water the soil of the plants from the top before you leave and allow the excess moisture to collect on the rocks. This simple solution will help prevent your plants from drying out for up to 2 weeks.

If you have a seedling tray with a capillary mat, you can press it into service for your houseplants. Place your plant pots on the wicking mat, pour enough water into the tray to fully moisten the mat, and allow the system to do its work.

If you're jet-setting to someplace tropical during the winter, ensure that none of your houseplants are placed near heaters or drafty windows.[8] —SN

*Spend some time setting up humidity stations for your houseplants before you board a plane to paradise. If you do, this Boston fern (*Nephrolepsis exaltata*) will still be luxurious when you return home.*

Why are water droplets coming from the tips of my plant?

Chances are you are seeing the evidence of transpiration in those drops of water at the tips of your plant's leaves or even at the top of a stem that has broken. It happens when a plant is saturated with water, often within hours of being fully watered. Literally, the plant is as full of moisture as it can hold, and the excess has to go somewhere. If it happens repeatedly after the plant has been watered, you may want to cut back on your watering a bit. The plant may be on the edge of being overwatered and all the trouble that brings.

Occasionally, those droplets are a result of a process called guttation. In this instance, the plant has caused its stomata to close, perhaps because it is nighttime, and the plant is resting. Or even if it is excessively hot, the plant may have closed down to prevent transpiration. However, if the plant roots are oversaturated, the upward pressure will force the plant to exude xylem sap (water plus nutrients) through hydathodes, which are literally pressure release valves or glands found at the tips or along the margins of leaves. This sap will taste a bit sweet, and if it drips on furniture, it may leave a mark.

Sometimes guttation can happen when a plant rebalances its levels of water and nutrients, often due to excess water in its system. Species in the Araceae family are especially prone to this phenomenon.

It is fascinating to see how plants can regulate themselves. All we have to do is monitor how we provide water for them and ensure that it isn't excessive.[9]—JM

Very specific—and interesting!—conditions create guttation in plants.

Hold Me, Feed Me, Love Me: Growing Mediums and Nutrients

4

What is the best growing medium for houseplants?

One that is fluffy (how's that for a technical term?), well-draining, and porous. It allows water to percolate freely but also retains it for use by plants. Generous air pockets in the soil allow the roots to easily grow and receive oxygen.

You can purchase potting mixes composed of topsoil and amendments such as compost, perlite, vermiculite, coconut coir, and peat. (Note that questions about the sustainability and environmental impact of peat and coir are heavily debated, and it is the gardener's choice as to whether they want to use these products.) Commercial potting mixes sometimes contain other ingredients such as hydrogels and synthetic fertilizers, so you'll have to also decide if you want to use these extras with your houseplants.

You can avoid the controversy and instead make a houseplant potting mix, using one part topsoil, one part compost, and one part perlite. Do not use soil that you've dug up from your garden as it will compact and turn into the equivalent of cement in your containers. As well, it may invite unwanted organisms from outside into your home.

Most houseplants will fare nicely with a good potting mix, but some have special requirements. Orchids, for example, can't perform properly in potting soil; they need special mixes to support them and offer the air circulation and drainage their roots need. Ingredients found in orchid mixes include perlite, vermiculite, sphagnum moss, shredded bark, expanded clay aggregate, cork, coconut coir, pumice, and rockwool.

Cacti also should be planted in a special growing medium that allows for the drainage they need. As they are desert plants, they are very drought tolerant. Straight potting mixes are simply too dense for them and hold too much water. They prefer a growing medium made up of a mixture of potting soil, sand, gravel, horticultural grit, perlite, or pumice. (If you're wondering what horticultural grit is, it's crushed limestone. You can substitute what is colloquially referred to as "budgie" grit, which is made up of crushed oyster shells. The most interesting thing about this is that it has recently been proven that budgies don't need grit to digest their food like some other birds, so the name is a bit problematic.)[1] —**SN**

Snake plants (Dracaena trifasciata) *can grow in mediums that by any other houseplant standard would be considered poor. They don't need a lot of nutrients or water to be successful.*

Should I sterilize my potting soil?

Many gardeners surmise that they can destroy fungi, weed seeds, insects, and other problematic soil denizens by pasteurization. Note that I didn't use the word "sterilize" here. A home gardener cannot truly sterilize soil—sure, you can use high temperatures to kill the micro-organisms in it, but your home environment isn't sterile. Outside of a controlled lab, you are only capable of pasteurization.

Jargon aside, pasteurization involves baking your soil at 180°F (82°C) for 30 minutes. You can do that in your oven or your pressure cooker, if you and your future dinner guests are okay with that. (At the very least, strong earthy odours may persist.) Understand that both beneficial and pest organisms will be destroyed in the process.

As I'm not a huge proponent of baking soil (I'd much rather make chocolate chip cookies in my oven), I try to purchase or create my own potting mixes from ingredients I know are uncontaminated. I never use garden or field soil in my containers, so I don't have to worry about my houseplants having risky soil. I make sure my tools and containers are clean and disinfected before planting.[2]—**SN**

Ensure houseplant health by practising good sanitation as well as using the highest-quality growing medium you can provide. This will help keep pests and pathogens at bay.

Should I put rocks in the bottom of my containers?

The short answer? No!

The reason we put rocks, gravel, sand, or even Styrofoam in the bottom of containers is to improve drainage. Or so goes the old lore.

The problem is that by doing so, we are going against the physics of how soil and water behave. Soil, be it garden soil or potting soil, absorbs water, which then drains through the soil profile by the agency of gravity. The water will saturate a soil layer, with the soil holding on to the water until gravity overcomes the strength of the bond between soil and water, allowing it to drain away into the next layer. In the case of pots, the water is held in that thin line above the intermediary level, such as rocks placed underneath the soil in the pot.

This rex begonia is in a nursery pot, which has excellent drainage. When you get this little beauty home from the garden centre, transplant it properly to ensure it continues to thrive.

The result is what is called a perched water table, when the saturated layer of soil is up closer to a plant's roots. That saturated soil can easily lead to anaerobic soil conditions and problems with roots rotting. It can also cause accidental overwatering if you tend to water until water comes out the bottom of the pot into a catchment tray. The perched water table can even interfere with airflow. Salts will accumulate in the intermediary layer rather than flushing through the pot, with damaging results to plants.

So, ditch the clay pot shards, rocks, and gravel, and fill your pots up with good quality potting soil. If a concern is soil escaping through the drainage holes, then line the bottom of the pot with a coffee filter or piece of paper towel. It works surprisingly well and doesn't contribute to that perched table.

Should you have a pot without drainage holes, don't plant into it directly. You can put a layer of rocks at the bottom, then pot up your plant into another pot with drainage holes and place it on top of the rocks. You aren't perching your water table because the soil level isn't in direct contact with the rocks below, and water will drain efficiently, and the air will flow easily. Do make a practice though of taking your potted plant out of the outer pot to water it, allowing the excess to drain through, and then replacing it in the outer pot. This will avoid excess water accidentally collecting below in the rock layer and becoming a potential issue.[3]—JM

Should I use hydrogels in my growing medium?

Water-storing crystals, water beads, and hydrogels are made from a polymer gel. The beads are sold in a dehydrated state but once hydrated will absorb 300 to 400 times their dehydrated volume with water.

Originally used to help in agriculture, they have been adopted in a big way by houseplant enthusiasts. Often they are added to the growing medium instead of perlite, to ensure that the medium is consistently moist. The beads also absorb nutrients and release them slowly, so any added fertilizer becomes slow release rather than a quick jolt.

Increasingly, the beads can be used instead of potting soil. Plants are literally grown in the beads, sometimes in glass jars that are very decorative.

As always there are pros and cons to using hydrogels.

On the positive side, they are excellent at ensuring that soil stays moist for those plants that should not experience soil that dries out between waterings. But that doesn't mean you can be haphazard at maintaining a regular watering schedule.

The beads also offer pathways for air as they shrink, providing aeration and preventing the growing medium from compacting.

On the other hand, the polymers are a known carcinogenic and neurotoxin. Care needs to be exercised when handling them, and they must be disposed of carefully. The beads are also a health risk for children and pets, especially if swallowed, since they will swell up and require surgery to be removed.

The beads may also exert pressure on the roots of plants as they compete for space in a pot. Plants may need to be repotted more often in increasingly bigger containers to prevent overcrowding.

Finally, the beads will break down if exposed to direct light, so they are best used with plants needing low light conditions.[4] —**JM**

Some mushrooms have popped up in my growing medium! Should I be alarmed?

They pop up seemingly overnight: tiny mushrooms, often in brilliant sulphur-yellow or silvery-white hues. You'll find them residing in the growing medium, nestled alongside your houseplants, and they're both cute and freaky all at once. Where did they come from, and what to do with them now that they've appeared?

Soil that is out in the garden—whether in containers, in raised beds, or in ground—contains countless species of bacteria and fungi. Your houseplants may inhabit the great indoors, but their growing medium still contains similar types of micro-organisms. Fungi are common components of potting soil, but you don't notice them unless they produce a fruiting body.

Fungi will prepare to reproduce when they are happy where they are, and if you spot them in your houseplants, it is likely a sign that you may be overwatering. Soil that is always damp is desirable real estate for fungi, so your main course of action is to stay the watering can a little. If the container your plant is in doesn't have good drainage, move the plant into a new home that does. If you are watering from the bottom, ensure that you are not letting the plant sit in a puddle of water for too long.

As for the mushrooms themselves, the species that tend to grow with our houseplants are usually toxic. If you have children or pets, it's best to oust the mushrooms by scraping them off the surface of the soil and discarding them. More will appear due to the extensive network of mycelium strands below the surface of the soil, but keep removing them and let the soil dry out a bit.—**SN**

My potting soil is getting crusty. How do I fix the problem?

Gradually building up over time, that crusty layer of yellow-brown or white crystals on the inner rims of containers and in growing mediums is a testament to countless waterings and fertilizer applications over the lifetime of your plants. Each one leaves salt and mineral deposits, which eventually pile up enough to become visible. If your tap water is hard, the concentrations of calcium carbonate and sodium are the main culprits, and if you use synthetic, water-soluble fertilizers, they leave trace amounts of residual salts after each application.

Unsightly, sure, but do these deposits actually pose a problem?

Yes, they can. They can cause plants to have difficulty taking up water and nutrients from the growing medium. In some cases, they may even alter the pH of the growing medium.

Bottom watering is an excellent practice with houseplants, but leaving water to pool in saucers at the base of the plant can be a big issue, and not just because it can promote root rot. It can contribute to the accumulation of salts in the soil, which may be detrimental to your plants' health down the road.

Fortunately, there is an easy fix. Flush out the growing medium by running water (hopefully water that doesn't have a lot of mineral deposits!) through the pot containing the plant in question. Bear in mind that if your container doesn't have drainage holes, this will be an insurmountable task, but your container should drain anyway. (See page 24 for the reasons why this is so important.) You may have to repeat the flushing process a few times for the best results.

If flushing doesn't work and the salt buildup is extraordinary, possibly encrusting the outside of the pot, you can transplant the plant into fresh growing medium.

Then, once you have a clean slate to work with, focus on preventive maintenance: do not use hard tap water to irrigate, and change up your fertilizing strategy so you are not using synthetic fertilizers. Don't let containers sit inside puddles in saucers for long periods of time. That just draws salts back up into the soil.—**SN**

I have grown cuttings in water. But can I grow some of my houseplants permanently in water? Which ones are best to do this with?

There is a fun trend among some houseplant growers to bypass traditional growing mediums and instead grow certain varieties of plants only in water. The aesthetics are pleasing with this type of growing, as you can use attractive glass jars or vases to showcase your plants. The fact that the sun shines through the glass and you have a view of your plants' root systems makes for eye-catching vignettes.

If you choose to grow your plants in this way, regular maintenance is necessary. This is a bit more work than growing plants in soil. The water in the jar must be changed almost daily—you can't leave it for very long or you risk harming your plants. Sunlight pouring through transparent glass jars may spur the growth of algae, so it may be useful for you to choose opaque glass containers.

As well, in this set-up, plants will not receive any nutrients from soil, so you need to be diligent about providing a fertilizing schedule. Once a week, offer them some water-soluble granular fertilizer (composed of natural ingredients) or liquid fertilizer. Dilute it according to the package directions, and take into account the volume of water the plants are growing in.

There are several plants that take a shine to growing in this way, including wax begonias (*Begonia* spp.), coleus (*Plectranthus scutellarioides*), impatiens (*Impatiens* spp.), philodendron (*Philodendron* spp.), and inch plants (*Tradescantia zebrina*). Why not experiment with this method, and see what you can accomplish?[5] —**SN**

Coleus is easy and fun to grow and propagate in water.

When should indoor plants be fertilized?

It often seems like guesswork as to whether our indoor plants need to be fertilized, as they don't exactly shout out their needs in the same way they do when we forget to water them.

Often, we fertilize when we think about it, regardless of whether it is the best time or not. Alternatively, we overfertilize, irrespective of whether the plants need the nutrients, which can lead to toxic conditions for plants. Either way our plants suffer.

*Umbrella plants (*Schefflera *spp.) need very little fertilizer to happily rock your living room.*

When we understand that our indoor plants follow the cycle of the seasons, even though they are inside with relatively static light and temperature conditions, it becomes easy to know when to fertilize. In general, our plants are not actively growing over the short daylight winter months. Come early spring, roughly two months before the average last frost, they are stirring and starting to grow again. During the summer months, they are actively growing, then starting to go into a low-growth cycle in the fall, and finally becoming dormant by the winter solstice. There are always exceptions, and you can recognize them when new foliage emerges even on the shortest of days, and you can respond appropriately. My zz plant (*Zamioculcas zamiifolia*) is a perfect example of being an oddball, as it sends up new stalks in January!

Start a fertilizing regime in late February or early March when you see your plants stirring and sending up new shoots or growing new leaves. Any fertilizer you use should be at half or even quarter strength, as your plants are still in the beginning stages of the active growing cycle. By June, most plants are in full active growth mode and should receive fertilizer at full strength. Then start to reduce the amount of fertilizer toward September and finally cease by December.

How often you fertilize will depend on the type of fertilizer you use. Liquid fertilizer should be applied biweekly or monthly. Granular fertilizers can be applied monthly or bimonthly. Slow-release ones should be applied only every three or four months.

However, in the end, it is your plants that will tell you which cycle they are following. My zz plant gets its first fertilizer of the year as soon as I see those first new shoots coming in mid-January, when everyone else is still sleeping![6] —JM

What are the best fertilizers to use with my houseplants?

If you've ever gone to a garden centre looking for fertilizer for your houseplants, you've likely stood in the (very long) aisle for several minutes, trying to determine which product will make your plants happy as well as be a friend to the environment. You may have an extensive collection of houseplants: Can you use the same fertilizer for all of them or do you need to buy several? How much of a dent will this make in your wallet?

Truthfully, you can make houseplant fertilizer shopping as complicated (and expensive) or as simple as you want, but here are a few guidelines to consider when faced with an aisle filled with choices:

Flowering houseplants such as this peace lily (Spathiphyllum wallisii) *need a regular fertilizer schedule to consistently produce blooms.*

1. Houseplant fertilizers are made from a variety of ingredients. Some are a man-made synthetic chemical cocktail, while others are made from delicious natural things like worm castings, compost tea, fish meal, kelp, blood meal, bone meal, and limestone. (It is easy to see which ones I prefer to use!) Fertilizers derived from natural ingredients will contain a wide range of macro- and micronutrients.
2. You'll find houseplant fertilizers in granular form or compressed into small "spikes" that you spear into the soil. Granular fertilizer usually needs to be mixed with water before application, while the spikes release fertilizer over time as you water. There are also liquid fertilizers. Liquid fertilizers need to be applied more frequently than granular types, but they are easy to use and chock-full of a wide range of nutrients.
3. What about slow-release fertilizer? These are usually a pelleted type of synthetic fertilizer, carefully designed to offer your plants small amounts of fertilizer over time. They do not have to be applied often, so they are easy to use. The slow-release aspect is appealing, but I will leave it up to you to decide if you wish to use them.—**SN**

I have compost and vermicompost at home. Can I use these on my houseplants instead of buying something from the store?

Absolutely, but bear in mind that compost and vermicompost are not fertilizers. We cannot measure the amount of nutrients they contain, and their composition will vary depending on how they were made. That doesn't mean you can't successfully use them, just that you have no way to know how potent they will be for your plants. If you choose to use compost or vermicompost, go very sparingly when applying it. You don't want to risk nitrogen burn or other issues, like insect eggs. —**SN**

You may need to experiment a little to find out what combination of fertilizers and amendments works best for each of your houseplants. Keep a record of your efforts so that you can compare results over time.

I've noticed that there are specific fertilizers for certain plants in the fertilizer aisle, such as for African violets and orchids. Is it necessary to purchase plant-specific fertilizers?

You can, but it's not absolutely necessary. Flowering plants have slightly different nutritional needs than plants grown strictly for their foliage. Flowering plants are typically offered more phosphorus (the middle number on your fertilizer label) than foliage plants are, but if you have only an all-purpose houseplant fertilizer in your shed, you can use that.[7] —**SN**

Propagation Preparation

5

Can I take cuttings of my houseplants to grow more plants?

Propagating our houseplants through cuttings is a great way to both have fun and increase our plants. The mechanism that produces an entirely new plant from just a piece of a plant comes down to meristem growing points in certain sections of the stems, leaves, and petioles of a plant.

Not all houseplants can be propagated via cuttings, and most can be propagated using only one plant part.

The easiest method is through a stem cutting. Simply snip off a length of stem about 6 inches (15 centimetres) long just below a growing node. Strip off any leaves below the top 2 or 3 leaves at the top of the cutting. Place the stem in a glass of water, ensuring no leaves are in the water, and place in a sunny spot. Do change the water every couple of days to remove any bacterial buildup. Within 3 to 4 weeks, you will start to see adventitious roots growing from the node and possibly the bottom of the stem. Once they are an inch (2.5 centimetres) to 2 inches (5 centimetres) long, it is time to pot the cutting in pre-moistened potting soil and place it in the light. Ensure that the potting soil remains moist until new growth appears at the top. Most species in the arum family (Araceae) will propagate through stem cuttings.

Some houseplants will propagate via stem cuttings directly in potting soil. Many succulents, including cacti, can be propagated using this technique. Start by removing a segment of stem from the mother plant and laying it on its side to dry, allowing a callus to form. Then pot it up in pre-moistened potting soil and wait for new growth. Christmas cacti are one of the easiest to start practising with before moving on to other plants.

Cane cuttings are a variation on stem cuttings. Take a section of mature cane or stem about 2 to 3 inches (5 to 7.5 centimetres) long with at least 1 growing node. Lay the section horizontally on the growing medium or stand it up vertically with the growing node above the surface of the soil.

A few houseplants can be propagated using a leaf blade. Remove a leaf from the mother plant and lay it down on moistened potting soil. Using a sharp knife, slice crosswise through a few veins to stimulate growth. I pin the leaf down so that it always has direct contact with the soil. (Straight pins from a sewing kit will do the trick.) Soon after, you will see a tiny growth forming at the site of a cut. Leave it to become established with both roots and stem forming at this point. Do not remove the old leaf as it will naturally disintegrate over time. Rex begonias (*Begonia rex*) are a perfect plant to try this technique out, as well as snake plant (*Dracaena trifasciata*) and peperomia (*Peperomia* spp.). ZZ plant uses a variation where the base of a leaf is buried in potting soil. Many succulents can also be propagated from a single leaf. Detach the leaf and allow it to dry for a few days, then insert the leaf just a tiny bit into potting soil. It takes a while for the new little plants to appear but don't despair. As long as the leaf remains healthy, the work is in progress.

Finally, you can grow new plants from a leaf petiole. This technique requires slicing off a leaf with at least ½ inch (1.25 centimetres) of petiole. Insert the petiole at a slant into moistened potting soil or perlite with the actual leaf standing free from the soil. After a while, a new plantlet will form at the base of the petiole just above the soil line. Allow the mother leaf to naturally die away. African violets (*Streptocarpus* sect. *Saintpaulia*) are the poster child for this method. But zz plant and jade plants, among others, can also be propagated in this way.

Growing mediums can be potting soil, perlite, sterilized sand, or vermiculite. My preferred medium is perlite as it retains moisture and air. Potting soil can get a bit too wet and may not have enough air but is generally successful if it is not too moist.

A rooting hormone compound is an option to assist rooting that will usually speed the propagation process up.

You can also enclose your cutting in a plastic bag to increase humidity around the plant part, but be careful to open the bag every few days to ensure that humidity levels do not become excessive and cause the plant part to rot. Once the new plantlets are well on their way, pot them up in the container they will be growing in from now on, adjusting the potting mix to suit their preferred soil.[1] —JM

*If you've never propagated plants from cuttings before, coleus (left) and holiday cactus (*Schlumbergera *spp., right) are two very willing candidates that will make you feel like a pro in no time.*

*Mother of thousands (*Kalanchoe daigremontiana*) naturally drops its tiny plantlets, which you can then plant into growing medium.*

Is it possible to propagate houseplants by layering?

Some houseplants naturally propagate themselves when they send out runners or stolons. Others, mostly vines, will root wherever their stems touch the soil. The trick with propagating these plants is to take advantage of their natural tendencies to deliberately make more plants.

Simple layering involves selecting either a stem, runner, or stolon and anchoring it down so that it touches the soil. I use bobby pins or floral pins, but anything will do the job from a small rock to a few paper clips. If I'm using a stem, I will slightly nick it where I want a new plant. Once there is a new plantlet growing strongly, you can sever the daughter from the mother and let it continue growing by itself. When it's a good size, you can transplant it to its new home. Spider plant (*Chlorophytum comosum*) is perhaps the easiest plant to try out this method of propagation. However, monstera, heartleaf philodendron, and string of hearts (*Ceropegia woodii*) are also good ones to hone your skill on.

Vines, such as English ivy (*Hedera* spp.) and golden pothos, can be propagated by compound layering, where stems are pinned down in multiple locations. New plants will then grow at each location.

Air layering, on the other hand, allows for propagation using a plant's tendency to produce roots at a growing node without needing a stem to be bent down and secured in potting soil. If you would like to propagate a dicot species in this way, cut all the way around the stem at a point roughly 12 to 18 inches (30 to 45 centimetres) down from the tip of the shoot. Then about 1 inch (2.5 centimetres) below, cut all the way around the stem again. Remove the bark in between. With monocots, simply cut a notch into a stem at a slanting angle about two-thirds of the way through. Keep the cut open using a toothpick wedged in.

Next, place moistened sphagnum moss around the stem and cover it entirely with plastic wrap. Secure the pad of moss and plastic wrap with tape. Keep checking the moss, making sure it is moist, and watching for roots to appear in the moss. Once the roots are well established, cut off the stem just below the roots and transplant the top of the stem with roots attached into its new home. Plants such as croton (*Codiaeum variegatum*), rubber tree (*Ficus elastica*), and weeping fig

(*Ficus benjamina*) are prime candidates for the dicot method; in terms of monocots, dumb cane (*Dieffenbachia seguine*) and dracaena (*Dracaena* spp.) work well with this approach.

Layering is an easy way to propagate houseplants as the plantlets are fully supported by the mother plant while they are establishing. However, it does take time and cannot be hurried along. No matter how impatient we may be to have layering work, we are operating in plant time, not our time![2] —JM

Don't be intimidated by layering! Try experimenting on Dracaena *spp.*

My houseplants are growing out of their pots. How can I divide them successfully?

My zz plants are in love with life, and I need to frequently divide them so that they don't actually break the ceramic pots they are in. They—and other houseplants such as foxtail asparagus fern (*Asparagus densiflorus*), cast iron plant (*Aspidistra elatior*), peace lily, spider plant, and pothos—are relatively easy to divide, and they usually rebound with a flourish.

Dividing houseplants is one of my favourite ways to propagate them. It's uncomplicated and a bit messy, which makes me feel like I've done something very rewarding. Get started by removing the plant from its container. My zzs will sometimes put up a fight because they are crammed so tightly into the pot, so you may need to take a sharp knife and run the blade along the inside edge of the pot to loosen the plant. When you pull the plant out of the container, you'll see obvious points where you can pull or cut the plant apart.

Then, it's merely a matter of repotting the divisions into new containers with fresh potting soil. Replant the parent as well, keeping most of its original soil and adding new potting mix as needed. Water all the divisions, but wait about two weeks before resuming your regular fertilizing schedule.

Plants such as African violets form offsets around the parent plant. These offsets can be cut away from the original plant using a sharp knife and can then be potted into fresh soil.[3]—**SN**

Plant patents

Every so often, you'll come across a houseplant in a store that has a label on it stating that propagation is prohibited. That means that the plant probably has a patent placed on it by a plant breeder. The patent makes it illegal for the purchaser to propagate the plant through various means, including vegetatively (asexually). That means you won't be able to take cuttings from it or divide it.[4]—**SN**

I would like to grow some houseplants from seeds. Which ones are good to try?

Growing houseplants from seed is an incredibly rewarding experience, primarily because most species take a long time to start and grow. If you're used to growing annual flowers or vegetables from seed, growing houseplants from seed is a definite marathon, rather than a sprint! It is common for houseplant seeds to take one to two months to germinate, and it can be a year or more before the plants reach maturity. It is essential to ensure that the seed beds stay damp while the seeds prepare to germinate, and your patience may wear a little thin while you wait. But if you're up for the challenge, here are a few varieties that grow well (if slowly) from seed:

- Bird of paradise (*Strelitzia* spp.)
- Dragon tree (*Dracaena draco*)
- Dwarf umbrella plant (*Schefflera arboricola*)
- Living stones (*Lithops* spp.)
- Ponytail palm (*Beaucarnea recurvata*)
- Swiss cheese plant (*Monstera deliciosa*)[5] —SN

Some of the most unusual houseplants are easy to grow from seed. Try living stones (top) and bird of paradise (bottom). Don't forget to bring your patience!

Righting the Wrongs: Dealing with Pests, Diseases, and Environmental Problems

6

Suddenly, some of my houseplants are dropping leaves. What is happening?

It is always shocking whenever our plants suddenly start losing leaves for no apparent reason!

We immediately think that some cultural malpractice has happened. Certainly, forgetting to water plants or the opposite condition, plants being overwatered, will account for the problem, and a simple check of the soil will confirm if this is the cause.

Pests and diseases also cause leaf drop. Look for signs and symptoms of various bugs that bug our plants, from mealybugs to spider mites and beyond. Likewise, various pathogens cause necrosis of the leaves, which will drop once they have died.

It could also be that you have overfertilized your plants, and they have gone into toxic overload from too many nutrients. Or it could be the opposite problem of forgetting to fertilize at all. Once the growing medium has exhausted its nutrients, the plants are living on borrowed time, and the first thing to go will be their leaves.

Exposure to extreme growing conditions will also do the trick. Widely variable temperatures, including opening the door when it is well below zero, can affect plants. Even just the proverbial battle over controlling the thermostat can influence sensitive plants. The low humidity in our homes will affect plants that come from tropical forests, though not the ones from the desert. Are the plants in question placed right overtop a hot air vent? If so, you have found the problem for sure!

Check the plants for signs of physical damage. Are they close to traffic, where we brush up against them too often? Or perhaps the pets have been snacking on them. Or children, for that matter. If they have been recently transplanted, there could be damage to the roots from repotting. If you have divided them, certainly there will be some shock to their systems, and down will go some leaves for a bit.

However, there is another cause: low light levels. Unless your plants are always under grow lights, there is a good chance that with the changing of the seasons, they are noticing the drop in duration and intensity of light with the coming of winter. This is especially true if the plants were outside for the summer months. Just as our outdoor plants go dormant for the winter, some of our houseplants will also do so. Usually within a month or two, they will start to grow new leaves. My croton plants are especially prone to doing this, and they live permanently in my kitchen bay window. Likewise, hibiscus (*Hibiscus* spp.) responds to the change of light by dropping leaves wholesale, as do many other species. But when they start to get that new foliage, it is time to cheer and celebrate the coming of spring.

All of which is to say that when plants are dropping their leaves, it is time to perform some diagnosis as to the cause. If it is a cultural practice or, heaven forbid, a pest or disease, then it is time for changes. If it is shock, for whatever reason, then it is time for some TLC until they recover as they will likely do so eventually. If it is the changing of the seasons, then go with the flow and ensure that your plants are well taken care of while in dormancy.[1] —**JM**

What are those tiny flies coming out of the soil when I water? Are they damaging my plants?

This may be the single most asked bug question Janet and I receive (what to do about flea beetles runs a close second!). Fungus gnats are pernicious and ubiquitous, but, fortunately, there are some simple ways to deal with them. I say "simple," but you'll also need a healthy dose of persistence and patience.

These tiny flies ($\frac{1}{16}$ to $\frac{1}{8}$ inch or 1.5 to 3 millimetres long) look a bit like slender fruit flies. You'll know you have a problem when you see them erupt in clouds out of the soil when you water your houseplants. (A single adult female can lay 200 eggs at a time, so you can imagine how quickly the population can explode.) Fungus gnats are attracted to the moisture in the soil, so if you like to overwater, you're just inviting them to hospitable territory. The larvae can burrow into the soil and munch on plant roots, interfering with nutrient uptake. Although the adults are not capable of doing much damage to plants, they are hugely annoying as they fly around and spread the love to other plants in our collections. At their worst, fungus gnats in both their larval and adult stages can transmit certain types of pathogens such as *Fusarium* spp., *Verticillium* spp., and *Pythium* spp.

In a word: Ick! If you notice fungus gnats, tackle the issue right away before they reproduce in the zillions. Smaller populations are much easier to control.

There are several ways to deal with fungus gnats. Eradicating the adults is the best option—if they cannot breed, there won't be any larvae to cause problems. The first thing you can try is to allow the soil to dry out in your containers. As well, provide a barrier on top of the soil: place a 1-inch (2.5-centimetre) layer of sand around your plant. You can use horticultural sand, if you have any, or even coloured play sand.

Sticky tape traps are easily available in garden centres and are inexpensive to purchase. They will attract and trap the flying insects.

Another option is to purchase beneficial micro-organisms called nematodes. *Steinernema feltiae* is one type that effectively parasitizes fungus gnat larvae. You could also try predatory mites such as *Stratiolaelaps scimitus*. They reside in the top few centimetres of soil. Both the adults and the larvae feed on fungus gnats.[2]—**SN**

What are Mosquito Dunks and Bits? Why would we use them for houseplants?

Mosquito Dunks and Bits (a brand name) are designed to kill mosquito larvae in small water bodies such as ponds. Great idea, you say, but what does that have to do with my houseplants?

Well, the products contain *Bacillus thuringiensis* subsp. *israelensis* (Bti), a bacterium that infects the larvae of mosquitoes as well as other winged insects such as fungus gnats and thrips.

The bacteria are harmless to plants, pets, and people and are safe to use in the water you use to irrigate your indoor plants. Simply break up a Dunk, which is sold as a solid disk, or sprinkle Bits, which are already broken up Dunks, into the water and let them dissolve before watering. Then drench the growing medium. The bacteria will kill the larvae of fungus gnats within hours and break the cycle of breeding. Use the treatment again in seven days and thereafter every two weeks until you no longer notice those pesky insects flying around you and your plants.

A word to the wise: Handle the actual Dunks and Bits with gloves and avoid inhaling the dust. Wash your hands thoroughly after using. Keep out of reach of children and pets.

A simple and elegant solution to a prevailing problem with plants indoors.[3]—**JM**

My hibiscus has lots of sticky sap all over it. What is bugging it?

You've got aphids. That sticky sap is an expellant from the insects (pretty much aphid urine—I sure hope you're not eating lunch right now!). These tiny soft-bodied insects slurp up liquids from plant tissues and, as they go along, cause plant stems and leaves to become distorted. A large aphid infestation can be very stressful for a plant and can sometimes be fatal. One of the tenets of Integrated Pest Management, which we're proponents of, is to closely monitor your plants on a regular basis. This gives you the opportunity to deal with problems as soon as you spot them. When you realize that aphids are causing an issue for your houseplant, take action right away. Aphids can usually be dealt with by spraying the plant with water. You'll have to do this multiple times before you get any results, so don't be discouraged if it doesn't work on one try. You can also put on a pair of soft gloves or use a soft, damp cloth to wipe the creatures off the leaves and stems of the affected plant. This can be a bit stomach-turning, but it's a great way to quickly eliminate a significant percentage of the population.—**SN**

This hibiscus clearly isn't suffering from aphids. But if yours is, nip the problem in the bud right away (pun intended).

What are all those little white insects flying around my plants? Why are the leaves sticky?

Whiteflies are the bane of many an indoor gardener. They are true bugs in the superfamily Aleyrodidae, which has some 1,550 species to plague you. Though chances are it is the greenhouse whitefly (*Trialeurodes vaporariorum*) that has its sights on your plants.

These are triangular-shaped white insects no more than 1/12 inch (2 millimetres) long with soft bodies. They are sap-sucking insects that excrete a honeydew everywhere from the leaves of your plants to countertops. They love to hide on the undersides of leaves, especially new growth, and lay their minuscule eggs there, too. But if you rustle your plants, clouds of them will fly up around you and the plants. You may also notice that your plant foliage has dull surfaces, wilts, turns yellow, or is dropping off prematurely. Plants can become stunted as photosynthesis is not possible with all the damaged leaves. If left unchecked, the infestation can quickly kill plants.

Time to take action!

The first line of defence is to give the top of your plants a good wash. I tip each container on its side in the sink and literally flush water all over the leaves and stems, which will remove eggs, adults, and the honeydew. Then I install yellow sticky traps around affected plants to see if the whiteflies return. If they do, I wash the plants again. If they are persistent, then I bring out a weak insecticidal soap solution to do the trick. But I keep examining the plants to make certain they remain pest-free.

In the meantime, confirm that you aren't giving whiteflies the ideal conditions to flourish. Mostly what they want is lots of new growth, so back off on the fertilizer for a while. Allow the soil to mostly dry out between waterings. If you can, put the plants in a cooler spot for a while as whiteflies love hot temperatures. To be safe, place the plants in quarantine. I make a tent out of floating row cover to surround the plants, but clear plastic bags will do the trick for a short period.

But if they just keep coming back or if the plants have been significantly weakened, you may have to lose the plants to stop the spread of these pernicious insects.[4] —JM

What is with the cottony-looking waste on my plants?

I would rather have any other type of insect pest than mealybugs! I know because at some point I have had them all, and, bar none, mealybugs are the hardest to control and eliminate from your indoor plants.

Mealybugs are scale insects but without the scale. Male mealybugs are tiny, gnat-like insects. Look for them floating in the air around your plants. Immature females are oval shaped and come in shades of yellow, pink, and orange. They are highly mobile and are starting to accumulate a fluffy, cottony white wax. Adult females don't fly, but they do have legs, so they can move around on plants. They are doing what all scale insects do—hunkering down on a leaf, or a twig, or an axil, to attach themselves to a plant and start sucking the juices out of it. To make matters worse, they excrete a sticky honeydew. Oh, and they lay lots of eggs. If left unchecked, mealybugs can cause a lot of harm to your prized plants, from damaged leaves that drop off once the life has been sucked out of them, up to, and including, plant death. They also will infect any plant around them as they are not fussy about their hosts.

We often get mealybugs from plants that have recently been brought into our homes. Do carefully check any plant you are given or have purchased for signs and symptoms. Mealybugs love warm and dry locations. My latest outbreak was in my kitchen bay window. A prime location.

So, what to do to get rid of them?

First, and it is hard to say, but if your plant is highly infested and is suffering from obvious damage, then you have to lose it. Quickly. But if things aren't so bad, start by placing the plant next to a cold window, as they really do hate chilly conditions. The bugs will move to the side away from the window where you can see them.

Then wash all the leaves and twigs, paying special attention to the nooks and crannies where they like to lurk, removing the sticky honeydew. If that doesn't do the trick, switch to using an insecticidal soap. Apply it to all parts of the plant. Wash it off thoroughly to avoid burning and other damage to the plant.

You will have to do repeated washings on a weekly basis to effectively remove eggs, nymphs, and females.

Should the infestation be tough to dislodge, step things up and use horticultural oil or dormant oil to smother the insects. A very stubborn infestation may require the use of an insecticide. If you choose to go that route, consult with an expert at a garden centre before proceeding.

It takes time and dedication to get rid of mealybugs, but, in the end, it is worth the effort to save your valued plants.[5] —JM

Hands down, mealybugs are top on our list of most reviled houseplant pests! Before you bring home plants from the garden centre or from outside, inspect them thoroughly to try to prevent these little terrors from spreading.

The leaves on my plant are stippled, and they are turning a weird silvery colour. They are also covered in tiny black spots. What is going on?

Here's another sap-sucking insect that pees on plants, in addition to causing unsightly distortions, silvery streaks, and spots of black frass on leaves, stems, and flowers. Thrips are thin, elongated, very small (about 1⁄25 inch or 1 millimetre) insects that can fly, although they're not good at it and usually jump when they are disturbed. Unfortunately, they're so tiny that you usually cannot spot them until you notice damage on your plant.

Thrips (and aphids, too, for that matter) can transmit pathogens from plant to plant as they move around and feed.

As with aphids, blasts of water can control thrips, and you can try wiping stems and leaves down with a soft, damp cloth. Foliage that is severely damaged can be trimmed away.[6]—SN

Thrips are a very common pest of both indoor and outdoor plants. That telltale stippling on plant leaves is a sure sign that thrips are present.

What are springtails? How do I know if I have a problem with them?

Springtails, also called snow fleas, are hexapods in the Arthropoda phylum. In appearance, they are small, less than ¼ inch (6 millimetres) long, with elongated bodies, and can be white or dark coloured. They are called fleas because of their ability to jump like fleas but are not the same thing at all.

Often springtails will appear outside as the snow melts, but inside they are attracted to moisture and love those houseplants that have excessively wet growing mediums. They are considered beneficial in the environment as they are microbivores and scavenge after organic matter found in soil and in decaying organic matter on the top of potting soil. While they are considered a minor nuisance, unlike other creepy-crawlies, they are not after your plants at all.

If you are a bit freaked out with them scurrying around in your pots, there are a few ways to lose them. Allow the soil in your pots to dry out as much as possible between waterings, then water deeply, and infrequently. You can repot the plants in fresh growing medium. You can also sprinkle diatomaceous earth on top of the medium. Alternatively, try to appreciate them and just let them be, as they will contribute to the health of the medium that your plants are growing in.[7] —**JM**

Should I consider using neem oil to get rid of houseplant pests? Is it legal to use in Canada?

You've probably heard of neem oil as an effective pesticide for houseplants, but it has a controversial status in Canada—as in, you probably can't use it for what you think you should be able to.

Neem oil is extracted from an evergreen tree (*Azadirachta indica*) native to India and South Asia. Uses abound (did you know that neem oil can be found in some toothpastes and soaps?), but what houseplant enthusiasts really want to be able to use it for is as an insecticide. Touted as a way to eliminate infestations of what I affectionately call the Big Four houseplant pests (mealybugs, whiteflies, aphids, and mites), the active chemical in neem oil, azadirachtin, can cause insects to stop feeding. It can also cause hormonal changes in insects, making them unable to lay eggs.

Here's the clincher, however: to date, in Canada, there are no products using neem oil that are legally registered as pesticides. Testing has not been done to determine neem oil's efficacy and safety as a pesticide. There is one product using azadirachtin that is registered for use in Canada to control the beetle emerald ash borer, but it is available only as an injectable and can be delivered only by certified commercial pesticide applicators. Many years ago, leaf-shine products for houseplants contained neem oil and could be purchased, but all these products were unregistered, and, in 2012, Health Canada removed them from the market. It is confusing, however, because neem oil isn't banned in Canada—you can easily source and purchase it, and it can still be imported into Canada without issues. You will read countless articles about how to use it to treat insect pests on houseplants. Off-label use is prohibited, however, so you'll have to make a decision about which side of the law you want to be on.[8]—**SN**

How do I keep my cats out of my houseplants?

As someone who has been owned by many cats over the decades, I can truthfully say that I have seen it all when it comes to cats and houseplants.

While most cats are not at all interested in your plants, no matter where they are placed in your home, there always is the one (or two or three) that is irresistibly attracted to them. Patrick, I have my eye on you right now!

It is important to realize when you hear a resounding crash and leap out to see your cat sitting in the midst of the carnage (or peering out from under the sofa) that they in all likelihood didn't cause the mayhem out of spite or ill temper. Cats are attracted to your plants because they are curious beings, and they are astonishingly clumsy at times. They also can quite like the taste of whatever is their favourite plant. They like the movement of leaves, the texture and taste of certain plants. Outdoors cats often gnaw at grasses, presumably to get some fibre to aid digestion or get that hairball moving along. So, hang your spider plant up high and place your dracaena out of sight if those are the favourite ones to chew as evidenced by their ragged leaves.

Cats can also get into your plants out of boredom. Or they could be anxious or stressed. Or want your attention. Providing stimulation of other sorts can be a remedy to their fixation with your plants. Or give them their very own plant to wreck or eat. I grow cat grass for my favourite chewer and always have dried catnip on hand for some extra excitement.

If you have a cat who wants to use the planter as an alternative to their litter box, then work to make the planter unappealing. Sharp pebbles can do the trick. I once resorted to aluminum foil over a planter that was a favourite. And skewers can work wonders too.

If there is a plant they simply won't leave alone, try a citrus spritz as cats really dislike the odour of citrus.

Finally, unlike the adage that you can't train a cat, but they can train you—there is hope that you can train your cat to stay away from your plants. It takes patience and perseverance, but it can be done. Patrick and I are still working on it.—JM

My plants have spots on their leaves, and the spots are increasing in size. What is causing this to happen?

When you find irregularly shaped tan, brown, red, or black spots on the leaves of your indoor plants, it can be a cause for alarm. Usually, the spots will start off small and circular with fuzzy edges. They will grow in size, and the middle of the spot will start to die off. Or if the spots are on a leaf's margin, they will grow in from the margin and turn black. Eventually, the whole leaf will be consumed and drop off, if you haven't pruned it off already.

Chances are your plants have leaf spot, which is not one specific organism but a collective name for a range of fungi and bacteria that can affect your plants.

All is not lost, though, as there are various management strategies that can help your plants defend themselves against the pathogen and recover.

Do prune off any leaves that are affected. Increase air circulation around the plants, perhaps with a small fan. Give the plants space to reduce humidity levels. Cut back on the amount of water to the minimum that the plants need to survive. When watering, make sure to do so early in the day, and ensure that no water gets on the leaves.

If the infection is persistent, you may want to use a copper-based fungicide on the leaves, but carefully follow the instructions, and ensure that the fungicide is safe for the plants in question. Some plants, such as ivies and bromeliads, are easily harmed by this type of fungicide.

Once the plants are in recovery mode, review the location where you have placed them and your watering practices to make sure that you aren't providing conditions that will stress the plants.[9]—JM

My plants are looking distinctly sad all of a sudden. What is happening?

When perfectly happy plants all of a sudden look worse for wear, it is usually due to being stressed. We look terrible when we are stressed and so do plants. Typically, leaves turn yellow or brown with black edges. Or they droop dramatically. Leaves will detach readily if touched or bumped. Flowers quickly fade and fall off. These plants just look sad.

Our diagnostic skills need to be deployed right away.

First, check for signs or symptoms of common insects and pathogens. If you discount that problem, especially if no other plants are affected, then check the soil for overwatering or underwatering. If that is A-okay, then it is on to the next step, that of growing conditions.

If plants have recently been repotted or divided, they could be facing transplant shock, if roots have been damaged. In that instance, you will need to wait it out, and hope that the roots will recover and the plants will become healthy again. Do provide ideal growing conditions in terms of light, water, and even temperatures. Do not fertilize!

Next up: Have plants been damaged through people bumping into them, pets chomping at them, or any other physical activity that has affected them? If so, then prune off the damaged leaves, and ensure that the plants get some TLC in terms of ideal growing conditions. Chances are they will repair themselves.

Finally, there is plant shock. Have the plants been suddenly exposed to new growing conditions? For example, have they been moved into a new location with different light? Or has the weather outside significantly changed, such as winter coming on? Have the plants been exposed to heat from hot air vents turned on with the colder weather? In the summer, if you have air conditioning, has it been turned on? Are the plants in the way of cold drafts from doors or windows being opened? If the plants are in a window, is the cold freezing the plants or the heat frying them? Have you recently fertilized the plants and given too much at one time?

If any of these variables have happened, it is time to find remedies. Some plants will recover slowly as they adjust to their new locations. You will just have to be patient. If it was a sudden chill or the opposite, then you may need to prune off some of the obviously dying leaves, and then give the plants time to recover. If it is a matter of drafts, then it's best to relocate the plants away from the source of said drafts. Be warned though that if any of the plants are very sensitive, they may not recover from chilly, hot, or drafty conditions. If the plants have received too much fertilizer, you may want to repot them with fresh soil.

In all instances, it is important to determine as quickly as possible the source of the problem. Like us, plants usually go on their way happily enough. A sudden change in their condition is definitely worth the attention we can provide, and usually they will recover over time.—JM

Dieffenbachia *is extremely difficult to bring to flower indoors. This one is obviously very loved and properly cared for.*

Why are the leaves on my plants browning and crisping?

Troubleshooting the cause of your browning crispy houseplant leaves can be challenging, but consider potential watering issues first. If you inconsistently water—allowing plants to dry out too much between waterings and not offering enough water (or too much one time and way too little the next time)—that may be the problem. If your houseplants need a lot of humidity and your house is dry and hot, adjustments are necessary to make your green companions happy.

And what about fertilizer? Too much fertilizer—especially if you apply it to dry soil—is a surefire way to promote crispy leaves. Watch how much fertilizer you offer throughout the year. You'll likely want to cut way back during the winter months or stop fertilizing altogether. —**SN**

Low humidity will often cause leaf margins to brown and curl. Sometimes the foliage will completely die back.

Why are the leaves on my houseplants becoming pale and yellow?

It can take a bit of detective work to try to determine why your houseplants have leaves that are turning yellow and pale, but here are a few possibilities:

1. Overwatering (did you anticipate I was going to mention that?) can cause root rot, which, in turn, can affect the rest of a plant, including its leaves. If you suspect root rot, transplanting the plant into fresh soil and controlling your watering is the best solution.
2. Underwatering (I'm being predictable) is another possibility. When plants become too dry, they may employ a defence mechanism to conserve what little remaining water is available to them. Their leaves will yellow and drop until water is applied.
3. Cold—whether it comes from a drafty door in the wintertime or a blasting air-conditioning unit in the summer—can be very hard on houseplants. When you are placing plants in your living space, consider their exposure to chilly air and put them elsewhere.
4. Insufficient light may cause leaves to yellow. You'll probably see the stems become leggy as well. At least the solution to this is easy (provided you have the space and a better light source!).
5. Your plants need new digs. Houseplants that are overdue for transplanting may suffer from yellowing leaves.
6. Nutrient deficiencies may be the culprit. If the older leaves on your plants are the ones turning yellow, it could be that your plants are lacking sufficient nitrogen. Fertilize more often with an appropriate fertilizer so that your plants get the proper nutrient balance they require.
7. When your plants reach an advanced age, according to their species, one of the signs that they are nearing the end of their lives is yellowing leaves. We often surmise that houseplants die due to our neglect, but sometimes we do a great job of looking after them, and they die after long lives properly lived.—**SN**

The leaves on my houseplants are chalky and dull. What do I do?

If your houseplants' leaves are looking a little less than lustrous, it is likely due to an accumulation of dust. Besides the fact that dusty plants aren't particularly attractive, dust can also clog the pores (stomata) found on the leaves, preventing the process of transpiration as well as keeping the plants from achieving optimal photosynthesis. Dust can also sometimes mask more serious problems, hiding evidence of insect activity until it becomes a huge problem.

Cleaning your houseplants requires time, a gentle touch, and an assemblage of specific tools. A soft cloth dampened with water is ideal to clean plants that have large, broad leaves such as *Dieffenbachia*. Soft cotton gloves and even a sock are also gentle ways to wipe debris from your plants. For plants that are spiny or succulent, or have long, thin leaves, other options such as toothbrushes, paint-brushes, and cotton swabs may be useful. Be creative and fit the tools to the types of plants that you have.

As for leaf-shine products, I'm not entirely keen on them. They may make your plants look like a million bucks, but the oils that they contain can actually block the stomata again. Likewise, don't do the mayonnaise hack—shining your houseplant leaves with this particular condiment will certainly give them the glamorous look you want, but there is a lot of oil in mayo. Save it for your potato salad instead. —SN

*Keep succulents such as this tree houseleek (*Aeonium *spp.) shiny by gently cleaning them with a cotton swab.*

Why are the roots of my houseplants rotting?

Almost without fail, the cause of houseplants exhibiting root rotting in their pots is incorrect watering, and usually overwatering. However, the cause can also be overcrowded roots in pots with less-than-ideal drainage.

Plants will start to fail with wilting and yellowing leaves. They will have stunted growth and likely fail to flower. If you dig deeper and check the roots, they will be soft, perhaps even mushy, and be not a healthy cream or tan colour but rather brown or even black. The roots may even smell funky. The problem is that the excessive moisture has allowed fungi or bacteria, likely either *Fusarium* spp. or *Pythium* spp., to set up shop.

Good news: this rubber plant (Ficus elastica) *does not have root rot. You want your plants to look like this, with firmly upright stems and leaves that are not discoloured.*

You have to work fast as almost certainly your plants will die if the problem is left unattended.

To try to save your plants, take them out of their pots and remove as much of the soil as you can. Inspect the roots, removing all that are decayed. If there are still a few roots that are healthy, then there is a chance. If the roots literally fall away from the crown of any of the plants and the leaves are affected as well, then it's a goner.

Assuming that the situation isn't that far advanced, continue to remove all parts of the plants that are affected. Repot the plants with fresh, moistened potting soil that has perlite in it for aeration. Ensure that the pots have really good drainage holes, where excess water can freely drain away. Make sure that you sterilize any tools that you use to prevent the fungi or bacteria from being transmitted to other plants.

Then leave the plants alone for about a week. At the end of the week, if the top few inches of soil feel dry, it is time to resume watering. If bottom watering, do not leave water standing in the tray. If top watering, water till the water comes out of the bottom of the pots and remove any excess that accumulates. You can also try using a 1-to-1 ratio of 3 percent hydrogen peroxide (H_2O_2) with water to irrigate your plants. It will kill any remaining pathogens on the roots, though it will not be able to affect any pathogens inside the plant tissue. Hydrogen peroxide also assists in oxygenating the soil.

Then, it is all up to the plants to repair the damage, rejuvenate their root structures, and be on their way to becoming healthy plants again.[10]—JM

Flowering buds are dropping from my plants. Why is this happening?

Bud blast, as it is called when your flower buds suddenly drop off otherwise healthy plants, is always upsetting.

Almost all reasons for buds vacating the premises, as it were, are down to the environment the plants in question are growing in and any sudden changes to it. The good news is that once you have figured out the cause, and you change the location of the plants or the care of them, they will soon be flowering beautifully again.

One cause is improper watering—typically underwatering or infrequent watering. Plants may then abort their buds, attempting to preserve energy-producing parts of the plants. Overwatering can lead to a pathogen setting up shop, often fungal in nature, that results in buds dropping.

Incorrect lighting, especially too low light, means the buds don't have the chance to develop properly. Temperature extremes, especially if they are all over the map, can be a cause, with plants going into survival mode. The first thing that goes is the flowers.

Low humidity is often a cause, as that dearth of humidity will literally dry the buds before they can open. Sometimes when the air is too dry, the buds can't even develop properly, leading to the same result.

Plants that have been recently transported from a store to your home will frequently lose flower buds as they cope with the changes to their environment. Some really sensitive plants will even do so if you move them to a new location in your home. Or even turn them around in the same location.

Plants that have been repotted or divided will also drop flower buds as they repair any damage to their roots and other structures.

If all of the above issues have been addressed and plants are still looking a little unhealthy, do check for thrips, as often an infestation will lead to bud blast. (See page 94 for how to deal with thrips.)

Assuming that at least one of these possibilities is an aha moment, changing up the location of the plants or your cultural practices, or giving plants time to rehome themselves, will have the happy result of your plants flowering well the next time around. —JM

*Christmas cactus (*Schlumbergera truncata*) is notorious for bud blast.*

My cactus is all mushy. What is causing this?

By the time a cactus becomes mushy, things have already been going wrong for some time. A soft, squishable cactus is suffering from rot, much like that avocado you failed to eat the very second it ripened.

A cactus with rotting roots may exhibit other signs of distress: it may be turning brown or yellow, particularly near the top, or the stems may be drooping. You may notice an unmistakable decaying odour.

A cactus with severe root rot may never recover, but it's always worth trying to save it before making the decision to toss it. Repotting it into fresh growing medium is the first step. (If your cactus has spines, be careful as you wrestle it out of the container. Wear gloves.) Inspect the roots, and if they are blackened and soft, trim away as much of the diseased tissue as you can without sacrificing all of the roots.

The next step may seem a bit drastic, but it's essential to getting the plant back on track to good health. Don't repot the cactus right away; instead, set it aside for a few days and let it dry out. The roots will callus, preparing the plant for repotting. Transplant your hopefully healthier cactus into fresh cactus-growing medium, and watch your watering habits from then on out.

Other causes of rot in cacti are fungal or bacterial in origin. Bacteria such as *Erwinia carotovora* will attack cacti, entering through physical wounds created by insect feeding and other agents. *E. carotovora* causes soft rot, characterized by slimy brown or black tissue and that mushy consistency we really don't want to see. Likewise, species of *Fusarium* (the same genus that causes damping off in seedlings) can be a major contributor to rot in roots and stems. Overwatering and a lack of air circulation make the whole situation worse—much worse.[11] —**SN**

My plant is leaning over. What is making it do that?

There are several reasons why your plant might pull a Pisa tower–like stunt.

1. It could be leaning toward a light source. This is called positive phototropism. Auxin (a type of hormone found in the growing tips of plants) creates more cells on the side of the plant that is in the shade, causing it to grow taller on that side. In response, the part of the plant closest to the light leans toward it. The cure is simple: move the plant into a spot that has more light. You can also turn the plant regularly to prevent it from leaning.
2. The plant could be suffering from root rot. If there is a chance that the plant has been overwatered one too many times and you are seeing other signs such as yellowing of leaves, it might be time to check the roots. You can do this by gently lifting the plant out of the container and inspecting the roots for blackening or browning tissue. You may smell a rank odour emanating from the roots. If this is the case, get some fresh potting soil. Prepare the plant for transplanting by trimming away the rotten roots (try to leave as many of the roots intact as possible as the plant will need them!). Repot the plant into the new soil and be judicious about watering. Hopefully, in time, the plant will recover.
3. If your plant is outgrowing the confines of its container, it might just develop a lean as the roots bulge and heave out of the pot. Transplanting is the remedy! —**SN**

How do I transport plants in cold weather?

The greenhouses are full of lovely houseplants in the winter months, just when it is the wrong temperature for them to be outdoors.

So how to get them from the store to your home safely is the question.

First, pick your day to shop. You really want the warmest temperatures you can get before buying them. Houseplants that are often tropical in nature and have been in the nice, comfy greenhouse will suffer chilling damage very quickly.

You and the greenhouse should be prepared to provide as much protection as possible. The goal is to keep the air temperature around the plants as high as possible. Wrapping the plants in paper or cardboard is better than plastic. Plants covered in plastic will lose warmth very quickly. And if it is below 32°F (0°C), then double wrapping is almost required as it will trap air between the layers of paper. If using a cardboard box, stuff paper around the plants so they won't tip over. This will also trap air around the plants.

Then make sure that your car is as warm as possible, and dash out to it. Try to place plants on the seats, not the floor as it is colder there. Head straight home. Do not stop for anything, and get those plants back in the warmth as quickly as possible.

With care and luck, your new plants will not have suffered on their way to their new home, but watch for chilling damage in the way of leaves withering, and if they do, then carefully prune them off.—JM

Flamingo plants (Anthurium andraeanum) *are a spectacular pick-me-up in the dead of winter, but you need to make sure they are properly bundled up for transport from the greenhouse.*

Let's Get Down to Specifics: More Tips for Success

7

How can I get my orchid to rebloom?

It would be lovely if our orchids would continually bloom! However, they usually need a period of six to nine months in dormancy to regroup for another round of blooms.

After blooming, do cut the old flower spike off, down to the first growing node. If the spike has turned brown, then snip it off at the base. This will encourage the plant to grow a new spike. Place your orchid in bright but indirect light and in a spot where the temperature will be between 65 and 85°F (18 to 30°C). Continue watering each week, ensuring that the roots are hydrated. Drain excess water out of the saucer as orchids hate sitting in water. Fertilize your plant once a month, with either special orchid fertilizer or one that is balanced between the three major macronutrients, but only at one-quarter to half strength.

Once your orchid has grown a fully developed new leaf, it is a signal that dormancy is ending. Now, place your plant each night in a spot where the temperature is between 55 and 65°F (13 to 18°C), though it still needs warmer temperatures during the day. This action will trigger the plant to send up a new flower spike. Quite honestly, if your plants (because you can never have just one orchid) are on a shelf near a window, just move them closer to the window where the cooler air at night will create enough of a temperature differential to stimulate reflowering. Just keep an eye on the outside temperature, especially if there is a cold snap or freezing conditions.

After a month or so, you should see what looks like an upward-growing root or bud on an old spike, resembling a rather knobby mitten. You have success!

Now, make sure to move the plant back from the window so it is once again in the temperature range of 65 to 85°F (18 to 30°C) and watch for the spike to elongate. Once it is 5 inches (13 centimetres), insert a supporting stick and clips. Boost fertilizer to once a week at half strength until the spike starts flowering. Then stop or reduce fertilizing to every two weeks at one-quarter strength.

Now, you will have blooms for a good three months until the dormant cycle begins again.

Do note that different species of orchid may require variations on this regime to rebloom. If your orchid is not reblooming, try changing up the intensity of the light it is getting, increasing the differential in temperature, making sure that it is never in a draft, and changing up the fertilizer to a higher percentage of phosphorus. Always ensure that the plant is allowed to dry out between waterings, and be patient. Maybe it just has to rebuild that energy needed to send up that flower spike and bloom again.[1] —JM

Moth orchids will readily rebloom under the proper care.

My orchid is dropping its flowers. What can be wrong?

There are several reasons why your orchid might be dropping its blooms, so you'll need to work through a process of elimination to determine what exactly is going on. This checklist of possibilities will hopefully help:

1. Your orchid is simply finished blooming. Most *Phalaenopsis* orchids, which are commonly found for sale at florists in North America, bloom for up to three months, then they go dormant for several months. During this time, they gather the energy needed to rebloom. Other orchids do the same thing with varying timelines.
2. If your orchid is dropping its flowers and the leaves are turning yellow, the problem may be overwatering. Check the roots of your plant. If they are black and mushy, the poor thing has root rot. Carefully trim away the infected tissue and repot the plant into fresh growing medium. This process is going to be very hard on the plant, so expect a delay in reblooming. Change your watering habits to boost the health of the plant.
3. Underwatering might be an issue. Critically observe your watering schedule and adjust it if the plant seems to be drying out too much in between waterings.
4. Orchids don't like cold temperatures or drafts. Consider where you have placed the plant in your space and move it, if necessary.
5. If your orchid is receiving too little or too much sunlight, it may prematurely drop its flowers. It is tricky to diagnose these issues, but if you've exhausted all the other possibilities, it may come down to light.—**SN**

My azaleas have stopped flowering. How can I get them to rebloom?

Azaleas (*Rhododendron simsii*)—and, for that matter, jasmine (*Jasminum* spp.), gardenias (*Gardenia* spp.), and cyclamens (*Cyclamen* spp.)—often seem like one-hit wonders when it comes to blooming. That's because all these plants need a few extra prompts to get them to rebloom.

Azaleas have very specific requirements: bright yet filtered light, high humidity, and consistently moist soil (don't let this houseplant dry out between waterings!). The ideal temperature range for them during the day is 60 to 65°F (15 to 18°C), but they need a nighttime temperature of 50°F (10°C) to initiate blooming. A monthly shot of fertilizer is always a good idea, too. Azaleas can have a lengthy bloom time, so if everything you've just done works, you'll have a gorgeous display of flowers over the winter.

Cyclamens go dormant after they flower and fare best if you place them in a shaded spot during this time. Don't let the growing medium completely dry out. When new leaves appear in a couple of months, move the plants into full sun and start fertilizing them monthly with a liquid houseplant fertilizer. Water them regularly. Temperatures matter with cyclamens, as well. Maintain the same range as you would for azaleas. With any luck, your cyclamens will rebloom shortly!

Jasmine and gardenias also need cool temperatures to spur on new flowers. Follow the same guidelines as for cyclamens and azaleas. Jasmine and gardenias also prefer bright, filtered sunlight, consistent moisture, and high humidity. These plants can be challenging to grow, but the satisfaction of seeing new blooms is immeasurable![2]—**SN**

What are those long sprouts coming from my monstera plant? What do I do with them?

Monstera and other epiphytic plants often form aerial roots. They originate along the main stem of the plant and grow quickly, giving your plant quite the jungle-like appearance.

These aerial roots are there precisely to provide the plant with a means of support as the plant grows up its supporting tree or structure. If you are using a moss pole, trellis, or other support to keep your monstera upright, then it is easy to train these thick brown protrusions around the support.

Alternatively, you can train the roots to go back down into the growing medium in the pot, providing additional support.

You can also cut them off. It won't harm the plant. Just be sure to use a sterilized, sharp blade and slice them off close to where they appear on the stem. They won't regrow at that spot, but be prepared for more roots to appear as your plant grows.

Once removed, there is no point in trying to propagate a new plant from them as they don't have the growing points or nodes necessary for generating a new plant. Just pop them in the compost.[3]—JM

How do I care for my African violet?

African violets are a group of about ten species with their native habitat in the understorey of cloud forests in eastern tropical Africa.

There they receive ten to twelve hours of filtered bright light each day and plentiful moisture, both of which are necessary for their optimal health in our homes.

Do provide your African violet with medium light, either from grow lights or by placing it in east-to-southeast-facing windows where it won't get direct sunlight. It is really looking for that ten to twelve hours a day of light, so if you don't have a good source of natural light, then grow lights are definitely the way to go.

African violets want their soil to be moist but not wet all the time. They also don't like their leaves and crowns to be misted or otherwise wet as they can then get leaf spot or rot. The easiest way to provide moisture is through bottom watering. Place the potted African violet in a saucer with water and let it soak for up to thirty minutes. Allow to drain and you are set to go until next time. You can also use a wicking pot, where a string or cord exits the drain hole in the pot and rests in a tray filled with gravel and water. The potted plant sits on top of the gravel.

Sometimes finding the right location in your home for your African violets can be a challenge, but once you do, you'll be rewarded with spectacular blooms!

The cord will wick up water when the soil in the pot above dries, ensuring the soil in the pot is always at an optimum moisture level. The extra water in the tray will also increase humidity around the plant, a nice bonus! Be sure to use gravel in the tray so that the bottom of the pot is not in direct contact with the water; otherwise, the soil can become overly wet and contribute to root rot.

Our African violets prefer a nice even temperature, somewhere around 65 to 80°F (18 to 27°C), which just happens to be the optimum temperature for our homes.

You can fertilize every time you water with a one-quarter strength liquid fertilizer to promote flowering. There are African violet fertilizers on the market, but you really just need a balanced (and preferably) organic fertilizer to promote good plant health and blooming.

Come spring, do aim to repot your African violet to give it some nice, fresh soil and a boost of nutrients. This also works to dissipate the salts that may have accumulated in the soil, which are very detrimental to African violets. Wash the pot to remove any salts that may have become encrusted onto the sides of it. This is also a good time to detach any pups and grow them as plantlets or even split your plant if it is getting too big.

Your African violet will reward you with being a long-lived plant that regularly blooms if you look after it. The only problem is finding enough space for all the ones you want to grow! —**JM**

Are asparagus ferns a fern at all?

The clue to whether asparagus ferns (*Asparagus* spp.) are actually a fern or not is in the name. Asparagus ferns are closely related to (you guessed it!) asparagus, but they are not a fern.

Whether it is Sprenger's asparagus (*Asparagus aethiopicus*), foxtail fern (*A. densiflorus*), common asparagus fern (*A. setaceus*), or lace fern (*A. plumosus*), they are commonly called ferns because their foliage resembles that of ferns.

But it makes all the difference in how we grow and care for them.

Asparagus ferns have fat, tuberous roots, and airy foliage called cladodes, with sharp scales at the bases. They thrive on bright, indirect light, away from drafts and cold windows. They love moist, rich potting soil and lots of humidity. I keep mine—and I have three different ones—in trays with pebbles. After popping the pots on top, I fill the trays with water to evaporate around the foliage. I also use a water globe or a clay olla to help keep the soil moist between waterings.

Asparagus ferns are tough. If they get out of control, or you just want to keep them in good trim, cut back individual stems to the base of the plants. You can also give them a flush cut right to the crown if plants need to be rejuvenated. They will come right back. I once thought one was dead and put it outside in the garden and forgot about it, only to find it flourishing at the end of the season with absolutely no care at all!

However, don't plan on harvesting any new shoots. Edible asparagus (*A. officinalis*) is the one to grow for those delicious spears![4]—JM

The frothy foliage of asparagus ferns is highly attractive. Consistent humidity is required to keep them looking their best.

How do I look after my cacti and succulents?

As a group, it is important to keep in mind that all cacti are succulents but not all succulents are cacti. Their care is similar but not exactly the same.

All succulents need lots of bright light. Mine are mostly in my sunny bay window facing southeast, and they flourish there. The rest are under LED grow lights that provide a cool white light. I keep the lights about a foot (thirty centimetres) above the top of the plants, and they apparently appreciate that light. Beware though that a too-sunny window can lead to sunburn on those leaves, especially if the window faces west and the plants are close to the glass. If you see dark patches on the leaves, then they are being burnt.

One of the most important things to do is plant up your succulents in pots with good-sized drainage holes. Do also amend any potting soil you use with coarse horticultural sand to improve drainage, as any growing medium that hogs the water will contribute to roots decaying and rotting in short order.

Succulents need more water than cacti as their thick, fleshy leaves transpire more than cacti. A sure sign that you are not watering enough is shrinking or shrivelling leaves. Overwatered cacti and succulents will have soft and squishy leaves and often the plant will drop them. What you shouldn't do is give them a little water every so often. The key is to allow the soil to thoroughly dry out between waterings. Then water thoroughly, allowing the moisture to go through all of the soil profile and drain out the bottom. Tip out excess water from the saucer so that they are not in standing water. In the winter months, you can go up to four weeks between watering your cacti. My succulents on that sunny window still need a good watering every week to two weeks, but I always check the soil before going ahead. In the summer months, you may need to water weekly, depending on how hot it is where they are situated.

While cacti and succulents generally prefer a lean diet, it is important to fertilize them when they are actively growing. Do fertilize on a regular basis during the summer months with a weak solution of a balanced liquid fertilizer. Cacti may need fertilizing only once or twice at this time of year and not at all in the winter. Succulents require more, in the order of three or four times during a longer growing period, but it is not necessary during the winter months.

Our succulents and cacti are generally not bothered by pests. However, mealybugs and scale can be an issue. Monitor for signs of their presence, especially if you have an infestation on other plants. Do also wipe the leaves of your succulents to remove dust and debris. I skip this step for my cacti!

It is seldom that I take my succulents and cacti outside, but if you do, they need to be in a sheltered and semi-shaded location, away from direct sun, winds, and hail. Variable weather temperatures are generally not what they like either. I am afraid mine are just pampered indoor plants![5] —JM

Seriously hirsute cacti like this one are unique additions to your collection.

Which houseplants are toxic to children and pets?

We certainly need to treat all our plants with respect, as almost all of them have developed some defences against being munched. Toxins in plants can be absorbed in a multitude of ways. They can be eaten and may upset the system when being digested. They can affect us simply be being brushed up against. Their sap can be phototoxic. Toxins can even be injected through sharp spines and thorns. Some secrete toxins into the soil. It pays to research the plants you have already and those you want to buy before adding them to your collection.

Most of the plants we call houseplants are perfectly safe for adults, children, and pets. But we should always respect their qualities and their medicinal properties. Some are mildly toxic, and you would have to really chow down on these plants' leaves, stems, or even roots to suffer more than an upset stomach.

But some plants have a high level of toxins and can cause serious, sometimes long-lasting effects. And a few can cause death quickly.

I have a houseful of plants of all sorts and three cats. Any of my plants that could be harmful to my four-legged critters are up high and out of reach of a determined animal. There are a couple of plants that I won't have in the house at any price.

Top of my hit parade (that is—plants I would never have in the house) is oleander (*Nerium oleander*). All parts of this plant are highly poisonous to everyone, and people die every year from ingesting the toxins, which are cardiac glycosides. Beautiful pink flowers make oleander a real temptation to buy, but I recommend never doing so in any situation unless you are buying for a conservatory, where there won't be any children or pets.

Sago palm (*Cycas revoluta*) and all cycads are highly toxic. They contain cycasin, which causes a whole range of issues including kidney and liver failure. The seeds (nuts) are the most dangerous.

Any species in the plant family Araceae contain insoluble calcium oxalates, which cause oral irritation, difficulty swallowing, burning sensations in the mouth and drooling and vomiting. Peace lily, philodendron, pothos, dumb cane, and arrowhead

(*Syngonium* spp.) are all in this family and are popular because they are tough houseplants that like low light. It pays to learn the botanical families of your houseplants as genera within them will have common characteristics as to the toxins they contain.

You wouldn't think that English ivy (*Hedera helix*) would be poisonous but its foliage definitely is, as it contains hederagenin, a glycoside, which causes hypersalivation, vomiting, and abdominal distress. Likewise, asparagus fern and all members of Asparagaceae cause problems as they have sharp scales that can cause allergic dermatitis.

A few plants may cause irritations if handled or brushed up against. Perennially popular zz plant is one such plant and is even poisonous. Mine is on a tall plant stand away from people and cats. Snake plant in the Agavaceae family contains saponins, which can cause nausea, vomiting, and diarrhea. Aloe also contains saponins, though the gel is a useful remedy for burns.

It isn't necessary to empty your house of all these and more plants that could cause harm to us and our pets. But if you do have a child, cat, or dog that just can't resist touching and eating your plants, you will have to put them somewhere safe from said critters. At the very least, eliminate those that fall into a highly toxic category, and choose ones that will not cause ill effects from enthusiastic sampling.[6] —JM

Arrowhead vine (top left), English ivy (top right) and aloe vera (bottom left) are plants to watch out for if you have children and pets.

Whimsical, unique, showstopping, adorable, collectible, therapeutic . . . we simply cannot resist houseplants!

Acknowledgements

From Janet and Sheryl: To be given the opportunity to write about growing houseplants is a dream come true for us! We cannot believe how fortunate we are! A huge thank you to our massively supportive, talented, and dedicated team at TouchWood Editions: Tori Elliott (publisher), Curtis Samuel (publicist and social media coordinator), Nara Monteiro (editorial coordinator), Paula Marchese (copy editor), Meg Yamamoto (proofreader), Sara Loos (typesetter), and Pat Touchie (owner). A very special thank you goes out to designer Tree Abraham for the stunning book cover and interior. And to Kate Kennedy: We are going to miss you so much! We cannot thank you enough for all your expertise, encouragement, and guidance as we've created books together these past five years.

From Janet: To all the indoor plants that have lived in my home, past and present, I thank you for all the joy that you have given me. To the other inhabitants of my home, Steve, David, and the cats, I thank you for not grumping at me when I bring home just one more plant! To Sheryl, my marvellous co-author and friend, thank you for all that you do for these books. We make a terrific team!

From Sheryl: Heartfelt gratitude to my family and friends, as well as all our readers and supporters—this can't happen without you! A huge thank you to Janet for our friendship and continued collaboration.

Notes

Introduction

1. Wolverton et al., "Interior Landscape Plants for Indoor Air Pollution Abatement," NASA (PDF); Jones, "Do Indoor Plants Purify Air?," LiveScience (website); Ro, "Can Houseplants Purify the Air in Your Home?," BBC; Wilkerson, "Houseplants Don't Really Clean Indoor Air," Harvard Kenneth C. Griffin Graduate School of Arts and Sciences; Lee et al., "Interaction with Indoor Plants May Reduce Psychological and Physiological Stress by Suppressing Autonomic Nervous System Activity in Young Adults," *Journal of Physiological Anthropology*.

Chapter One

1. Melrose and Normandeau, *The Houseplanter: Your Go-To Growing Journal*.

2. Davidson, *Doctor Houseplant*, 137.

3. Steil, "Moving Indoor Plants Outside for the Summer," Iowa State University Extension and Outreach.

Chapter Two

1. Avis-Riordan, "The Wardian Case: Botany Game Changer," Royal Botanic Gardens Kew (website).

2. Brain, "The Wardian Case," Historic UK (website).

3. Kelley, "Repotting Houseplants," PennState Extension.

Chapter Three

1. University of Maryland Extension, "Lighting for Indoor Plants"; Jabbour, "Understanding Light for Houseplants," Savvy Gardening (website).

2. Sears, "Do Grow Lights Work?," The Spruce (website).

3. Wolke, "Chlorine Confusion," *Washington Post*.

4. Pavlis, "Is Tea a Good Fertilizer for Houseplants?," Garden Myths (website); *Guardian*, "Gardens: Old Wives' Tales."

5. Davidson, *Doctor Houseplant*, 139.

6. Lipford, "Tips on Using Houseplant Watering Globes," Today's Homeowner (website).

7. South and Jones, "Watering Phalaenopsis Orchids with Ice Cubes," The Ohio State University, College of Food, Agricultural, and Environmental Sciences.

8. Langton and Ray, *Root, Nurture, Grow*, 107–8.

9. Plantura (website), "Guttation in Plants."

Chapter Four

1. McIntosh, "Choosing the Right Orchid Growing Material," The Spruce (website); Sears, "What Is Cactus Soil and How Does It Differ from Regular Potting Mix?," The Spruce (website); Rich et al., "Budgies—Feeding," VCA Canada Animal Hospitals (website).

2. Pavlis, "Sterile Soil—Does It Really Exist?," Garden Myths (website).

3. Cue, "The Hard Truth about Rocks at the Bottom of Planting Containers," University of Nebraska-Lincoln, Institute of Agriculture and Natural Resources, Nebraska Extension in Dodge County.

4. Antosh, "What Are the Pros and Cons of Using Water Beads for Plants?," Plant Care Today (website).

5. McIntosh, "33 Plants That Can Grow in Water Indoors," The Spruce (website).

6. Walliser, "Houseplant Fertilizer Basics," Savvy Gardening (website).

7. Walliser, "Houseplant Fertilizer Basics," Savvy Gardening (website).

Chapter Five

1. University of Missouri Extension, "Home Propagation of Houseplants"; Lerner and Welch-Keesey, "New Plants from Cuttings," Purdue University, Indiana Yard and Garden—Purdue Consumer Horticulture; Steil, "How to Propagate Houseplants by Leaf Petiole Cuttings," Iowa State University Extension and Outreach.

2. Kelley, "Propagating Houseplants," PennState Extension; Steil, "How to Propagate Houseplants by Air Layering and Simple Layering," Iowa State University Extension and Outreach.

3. Steil, "How to Propagate Houseplants by Division and Offsets," Iowa State University Extension and Outreach.

4. Whiteacre, "Propagating Your Plants Might Be Illegal—Here's What You Should Know," *Better Homes and Gardens* (website).

5. Smith, "14 Popular Houseplants You Can Grow From Seed," Plantflix (website).

Chapter Six

1. Iowa State University Extension and Outreach, "Several Houseplants That Were Brought Indoors in Fall Are Dropping Leaves. Why?"; Vanzile, "Why Leaf Drop Occurs on Houseplants and What to Do about It," The Spruce (website).

2. Arbico Organics (website), "Fungus Gnats."

3. Burnett, "How to Identify and Get Rid of Fungus Gnats," *The Old Farmer's Almanac* (website).

4. WallyGrow (website), "How to Get Rid of Whiteflies on Houseplants"; Burnett, "Natural Ways to Prevent Whitefly Infestations," *The Old Farmer's Almanac* (website).

5. University of New Hampshire Extension, "How Do You Get Rid of Mealy-bugs on Houseplants?"; Sproule, "Household Pest Control: Mealy Bugs," Salisbury Greenhouse (website).

6. Lupo, "How to Get Rid of Thrips," The Spruce (website).

7. UK Houseplants (website), "Springtails."

8. CBC Radio (podcast), "Gardening: Is Neem Oil Banned?"

9. University of Maryland Extension, "Fungal Leaf Spots on Indoor Plants."

10. Pino, "Root Rot Guide," Planet Natural Center (website); Grant, "How to Use Hydrogen Peroxide in the Garden," Gardening Know How (website).

11. Succulents Box (website), "How to Save a Rotting Cactus."

Chapter Seven

1. Dickson, "How to Get an Orchid to Rebloom—Expert Tips for Bountiful Blooms," Homes & Gardens (website).

2. Janousek Florist (website), "Caring for Your Indoor Azalea Plant."

3. Johnstone, "Monstera Aerial Roots: 7 Things to Know about Them," The Spruce (website).

4. Neveln, "How to Grow and Care for Asparagus Fern," *Better Homes and Gardens* (website).

5. Brown, "Cacti and Succulents," University of Minnesota Extension.

6. American Society for Prevention of Cruelty to Animals, "Poisonous Plants"; Canadian Child Care Federation, "Toxic Plant List."

Sources

American Society for Prevention of Cruelty to Animals. "Poisonous Plants." Accessed May 30, 2024. aspca.org/pet-care/animal-poison-control/toxic-and-non-toxic-plants/a?page=2.

Antosh, Gary. "What Are the Pros and Cons of Using Water Beads for Plants?" Plant Care Today (website). Accessed April 1, 2024. plantcaretoday.com/water-beads-for-plants.html.

Arbico Organics (website). "Fungus Gnats." Accessed April 1, 2024. arbico-organics.com/category/pest-solver-guide-fungus-gnats.

Avis-Riordan, Katie. "The Wardian Case: Botany Game Changer." Royal Botanic Gardens Kew (website). December 6, 2019. kew.org/read-and-watch/how-wardian-case-changed-botanical-world.

Brain, Jessica. "The Wardian Case." Historic UK (website). Accessed April 1, 2024. historic-uk.com/CultureUK/Wardian-Case/.

Brown, Deborah L. "Cacti and Succulents." University of Minnesota Extension. Last updated 2018. extension.umn.edu/houseplants/cacti-and-succulents.

Burnett, Christopher. "How to Identify and Get Rid of Fungus Gnats." *The Old Farmer's Almanac* (website). Last updated November 29, 2023. almanac.com/pest/fungus-gnats.

——."Natural Ways to Prevent Whitefly Infestations." *The Old Farmer's Almanac* (website). Last updated March 26, 2024. almanac.com/pest/whiteflies.

Canadian Child Care Federation. "Toxic Plant List." Accessed May 30, 2024. cccf-fcsge.ca/ece-resources/topics/child-health-safety-environment/toxic-plant-list/.

CBC Radio (podcast). "Gardening: Is Neem Oil Banned?" 2016. cbc.ca/player/play/1.3643732.

Cue, Kathleen. "The Hard Truth about Rocks at the Bottom of Planting Containers." University of Nebraska-Lincoln, Institute of Agriculture and Natural Resources, Nebraska Extension in Dodge County. Accessed April 1, 2024. extension.unl.edu/statewide/dodge/the-hard-truth-about-rocks-at-the-bottom-of-planting-containers/.

Davidson, William. *Doctor Houseplant: An Indispensable Guide to Keeping Your Houseplants Happy and Healthy*. Brentwood, TN: Cool Springs Press, 2020.

Dickson, Chiana. "How to Get an Orchid to Rebloom—Expert Tips for Bountiful Blooms." Homes & Gardens (website). January 8, 2023. homesandgardens.com/gardens/how-to-get-an-orchid-to-rebloom.

Grant, Amy. "How to Use Hydrogen Peroxide in the Garden." Gardening Know How (website). Last updated January 5, 2024. gardeningknowhow.com/garden-how-to/soil-fertilizers/using-hydrogen-peroxide-in-garden.htm.

Guardian. "Gardens: Old Wives' Tales." January 8, 2011. theguardian.com/lifeandstyle/2011/jan/08/old-wives-tales-gardens.

Iowa State University Extension and Outreach. "Several Houseplants That Were Brought Indoors in Fall Are Dropping Leaves. Why?" Last updated February 26, 2022. yardandgarden.extension.iastate.edu/faq/several-houseplants-were-brought-indoors-fall-are-dropping-leaves-why.

Jabbour, Niki. "Understanding Light for Houseplants: Types of Light and How to Measure It." Savvy Gardening (website). Accessed April 1, 2024. savvygardening.com/light-for-house-plants/.

Janousek Florist (website). "Caring for Your Indoor Azalea Plant." June 7, 2016. omaha-florist.com/flowers/blogs/Indoor-Azalea-Plants/.

Johnstone, Gemma. "Monstera Aerial Roots: 7 Things to Know about Them." The Spruce (website). Last updated March 20, 2024. thespruce.com/monstera-aerial-roots-6828242.

Jones, Lawrie. "Do Indoor Plants Purify Air?" LiveScience (website). December 9, 2021. livescience.com/do-indoor-plants-purify-air.

Kelley, Kathy. "Propagating Houseplants." PennState Extension. Updated March 14, 2023. extension.psu.edu/propagating-houseplants.

——. "Repotting Houseplants." PennState Extension. Last updated March 14, 2023. extension.psu.edu/repotting-houseplants.

Langton, Caro, and Rose Ray. *Root, Nurture, Grow: The Essential Guide to Propagating and Sharing Houseplants*. London: Quadrille Publishing, 2018.

Lee, Min-sun, Juyoung Lee, Bum-Jin Park, and Yoshifumi Miyazaki. "Interaction with Indoor Plants May Reduce Psychological and Physiological Stress by Suppressing Autonomic Nervous System Activity in Young Adults: A Randomized Crossover Study." *Journal of Physiological Anthropology*. April 28, 2015. ncbi.nlm.nih.gov/pmc/articles/PMC4419447/.

Lerner, Rosie, and Mary Welch-Keesey. "New Plants from Cuttings." Purdue University, Indiana Yard and Garden—Purdue Consumer Horticulture. Accessed April 1, 2024. purdue.edu/hla/sites/yardandgarden/extpub/new-plants-from-cuttings-text-only/.

Lipford, Danny. "Tips on Using Houseplant Watering Globes." Today's Homeowner (website). Last updated April 18, 2024. todayshomeowner.com/lawn-garden/guides/tips-on-how-to-use-houseplant-watering-globes/.

Lupo, Lisa Jo. "How to Get Rid of Thrips." The Spruce (website). Last updated January 5, 2022. thespruce.com/take-control-of-thrips-2656317.

McIntosh, Jamie. "Choosing the Right Orchid Growing Material." The Spruce (website). Last updated September 9, 2022. thespruce.com/choose-orchid-growing-media-1315968.

——. "33 Plants That Can Grow in Water Indoors." The Spruce (website). Last updated March 8, 2024. thespruce.com/houseplants-grown-in-water-4177520.

Melrose, Janet, and Sheryl Normandeau. *The Houseplanter: Your Go-To Growing Journal*. Victoria: TouchWood Editions, 2025.

Neveln, Viveka. "How to Grow and Care for Asparagus Fern." *Better Homes and Gardens* (website). Last updated March 24, 2023. bhg.com/gardening/plant-dictionary/houseplant/asparagus-fern/.

Pavlis, Robert. "Is Tea a Good Fertilizer for Houseplants?" Garden Myths (website). Accessed April 1, 2024. gardenmyths.com/tea-fertilizer-for-houseplants/.

———. "Sterile Soil—Does It Really Exist?" Garden Myths (website). Accessed April 1, 2024. gardenmyths.com/sterile-soil-really-exist/#:~:text=is%20not%20sterile.-,The%20Sterile%20Soil%20Myth,myth%20%E2%80%93%20it%20does%20not%20exist.

Pino, Melissa. "Root Rot Guide: How to Identify, Treat and Prevent Root Rot in Plants." Planet Natural Research Center (website). August 24, 2023. planetnatural.com/root-rot/.

Plantura (website). "Guttation in Plants: What Causes Water Droplets on Indoor Plant Leaves?" Accessed April 1, 2024. plantura.garden/uk/green-living/knowledge/guttation.

Rich, Gregory, Laurie Hess, and Rick Axelson. "Budgies—Feeding." VCA Canada Animal Hospitals (website). Accessed April 1, 2024. vcacanada.com/know-your-pet/budgies-feeding.

Ro, Christine. "Can Houseplants Purify the Air in Your Home?" BBC. July 20, 2023. bbc.com/news/business-66186492.

Sears, Cori. "Do Grow Lights Work? Everything You Need to Know." The Spruce (website). Last updated August 19, 2023. thespruce.com/how-to-use-grow-lights-for-indoor-plants-5221241.

———. "What Is Cactus Soil and How Does It Differ from Regular Potting Mix?" The Spruce (website). Last updated March 5, 2024. thespruce.com/what-is-cactus-soil-5113988.

Smith, Alina. "14 Popular Houseplants You Can Grow From Seed." Plantflix (website). April 22, 2021. plantflix.com/blogs/news/14-popular-houseplants-you-can-grow-from-seed.

South, Kaylee, and Michelle Jones. "Watering Phalaenopsis Orchids with Ice Cubes." The Ohio State University, College of Food, Agricultural, and Environmental Sciences. July 12, 2018. u.osu.edu/greenhouse/2018/07/12/watering-phalaenopsis-orchids-with-ice-cubes/.

Sproule, Rob. "Household Pest Control: Mealy Bugs." Salisbury Greenhouse (website). Accessed April 1, 2024. salisburygreenhouse.com/mealy-bugs/.

Steil, Aaron. "How to Propagate Houseplants by Air Layering and Simple Layering." Iowa State University Extension and Outreach. Last reviewed December 2023. yardandgarden.extension.iastate.edu/how-to/how-propagate-houseplants-air-layering-and-simple-layering.

———. "How to Propagate Houseplants by Division and Offsets." Iowa State University Extension and Outreach. Last reviewed December 2023. yardandgarden.extension.iastate.edu/how-to/how-propagate-houseplants-division-and-offsets.

——. "How to Propagate Houseplants by Leaf Petiole Cuttings." Iowa State University Extension and Outreach. Last reviewed December 2023. yardandgarden .extension.iastate.edu/how-to/how-propagate-houseplants-leaf-petiole-cuttings.

——. "Moving Indoor Plants Outside for the Summer." Iowa State University Extension and Outreach. Last reviewed December 2022. yardandgarden.extension .iastate.edu/how-to/moving-indoor-plants-outside-summer.

Succulents Box (website). "How to Save a Rotting Cactus." Accessed April 1, 2024. succulentsbox.com/blogs/blog/how-to-save-a-rotting-cactus#:~:text=Soft%20rot%20 caused%20by%20Erwinia,rapidly%20through%20the%20plant%20tissues.

UK Houseplants (website). "Springtails." Accessed April 1, 2024. ukhouseplants .com/pests/springtails.

University of Maryland Extension. "Fungal Leaf Spots on Indoor Plants." Last updated March 13, 2023. extension.umd.edu/resource/fungal-leaf-spots-indoor-plants/.

——. "Lighting for Indoor Plants." Last updated March 10, 2023. extension .umd.edu/resource/lighting-indoor-plants/.

University of Missouri Extension. "Home Propagation of Houseplants." Reviewed May 2022. extension.missouri.edu/publications/g6560.

University of New Hampshire Extension. "How Do You Get Rid of Mealybugs on Houseplants?" December 23, 2020. extension.unh.edu/blog/2020/12/how-do-you -get-rid-mealybugs-houseplants.

Vanzile, Jon. "Why Leaf Drop Occurs on Houseplants and What to Do about It." The Spruce (website). Last updated April 8, 2021. thespruce.com/leaves-falling-off -houseplant-1902676.

Walliser, Jessica. "Houseplant Fertilizer Basics: How and When to Feed Houseplants." Savvy Gardening (website). Accessed April 1, 2024. savvygardening.com /houseplant-fertilizer/.

WallyGrow (website). "How to Get Rid of Whiteflies on Houseplants." October 2, 2020. wallygrow.com/blogs/feature/whiteflies.

Whiteacre, Benjamin. "Propagating Your Plants Might Be Illegal—Here's What You Should Know." *Better Homes and Gardens* (website). October 28, 2022. bhg.com/what-is-a-plant-patent-6823149.

Wilkerson, Jordan. "Houseplants Don't Really Clean Indoor Air." Harvard Kenneth C. Griffin Graduate School of Arts and Sciences. November 19, 2019. sitn.hms .harvard.edu/flash/2019/house-plants-dont-really-clean-indoor-air/.

Wolke, Robert L. "Chlorine Confusion." *Washington Post*. January 22, 2003. washingtonpost.com/archive/lifestyle/food/2003/01/22/chlorine-confusion/ea7f000b -fe25-4385-85d0-021e33679ae7/.

Wolverton, B.C., Anne Johnson, and Keith Bounds. "Interior Landscape Plants for Indoor Air Pollution Abatement." NASA (PDF). September 15, 1989. ntrs.nasa.gov /citations/19930073077.

Index

Page numbers in italics refer to photographs.

© *Steve Melrose*

About the Authors

SHERYL NORMANDEAU was born and raised in the Peace Country region of northern Alberta and has made Calgary her home since 1994. A writer and master gardener, Sheryl holds a bachelor's degree in English, as well as a Prairie Horticulture Certificate and an Urban Sustainable Agriculture Certificate. Between 2013 and 2023, she served as the online Ask an Expert for the Calgary Horticultural Society. She works at the Calgary Public Library—besides gardening, books of all kinds are her grand passion! She is a small-space gardener (on a tiny balcony and in a plot in a nearby community garden), and she is most enthusiastic about growing veggies. She lives with her husband, Rob, and their rescue cat, Smudge. Find Sheryl at Flowery Prose (floweryprose.com) and on Facebook (@FloweryProse1), X (@Flowery_Prose), and Instagram (flowery_prose).

JANET MELROSE was born in Trinidad, West Indies, and immigrated to Canada in 1964. She has lived in Calgary since 1969. She is a master gardener and the creator and owner of the successful horticulture business Calgary's Cottage Gardener, which specializes in garden education and consultation, horticultural therapy, and advocating for sustainable local food systems. She holds bachelor's degrees in sociology and history, a Prairie Horticulture Certificate, and a Horticultural Therapy Certificate. Janet is a lifelong gardener, coming from a heritage of English gardening. She has a large garden at home in the suburbs of Calgary that can only be described as a typical cottage garden. She cares for many other gardens throughout Calgary through her work as a horticultural therapist, as well as a bed at the Inglewood Community Garden. She is married to Steve and has two children, Jennifer and David. Three cats, Patrick, Theo, and Mia, currently own their home and patrol against the deer, hares, squirrels, skunk, mice, insects, and assorted birds that believe the garden is theirs, too! Connect with Janet on Facebook (@Calgarys-Cottage-Gardener), X (@CalCottageGrdnr), and Instagram (CalgarysCottageGardener).

Books by Janet Melrose and Sheryl Normandeau

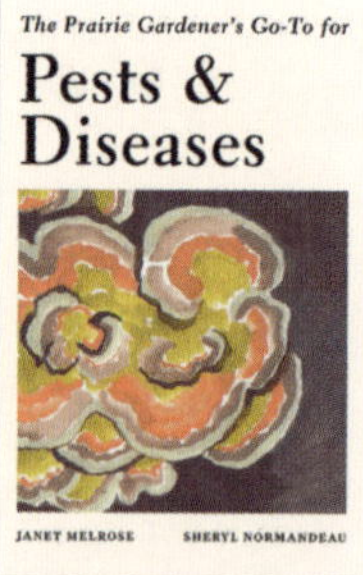

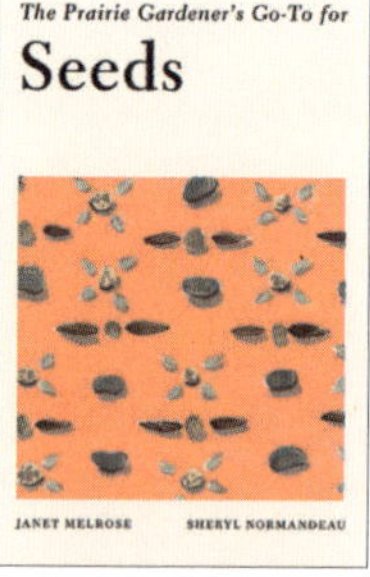

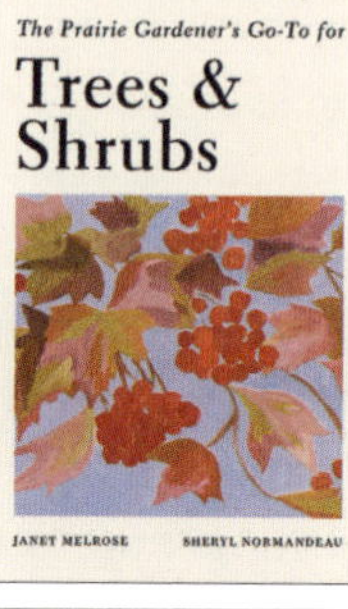